INTERNET THEORY, TECHNOLOGY AND APPLICATIONS

CYBERSECURITY AND CYBER-INFORMATION SHARING

LEGAL AND ECONOMIC ANALYSES

INTERNET THEORY, TECHNOLOGY AND APPLICATIONS

Additional books in this series can be found on Nova's website under the Series tab.

Additional e-books in this series can be found on Nova's website under the e-book tab.

INTERNET THEORY, TECHNOLOGY AND APPLICATIONS

CYBERSECURITY AND CYBER-INFORMATION SHARING

LEGAL AND ECONOMIC ANALYSES

JULIA M. MORGAN
EDITOR

nova publishers
New York

Library of Congress Cataloging-in-Publication Data

ISBN: 978-1-63483-137-6

Published by Nova Science Publishers, Inc. † New York

CONTENTS

PREFACE

Over the course of the last year, a host of cyberattacks has been perpetrated on a number of high profile American companies. The high profile cyberattacks of 2014 and early 2015 appear to be indicative of a broader trend: the frequency and ferocity of cyberattacks are increasing, posing grave threats to the national interests of the United States. While considerable debate exists with regard to the best strategies for protecting America's various cyber-systems and promoting cybersecurity, one point of general agreement amongst cyber-analysts is the perceived need for enhanced and timely exchange of cyber-threat intelligence both within the private sector and between the private sector and the government. This book examines the various legal issues that arise with respect to the sharing of cybersecurity intelligence, with a special focus on two distinct concepts: (1) sharing of cyberinformation within the government's possession and (2) sharing of cyber-information within the possession of the private sector. Furthermore, the authors analyze the incentives for companies to share information about cybersecurity breaches with other companies and the federal government, and conclude with a discussion on several bills passed on information sharing in cybersecurity.

In: Cybersecurity and Cyber-Information Sharing ISBN: 978-1-63483-137-6
Editor: Julia M. Morgan

Chapter 1

CYBERSECURITY AND INFORMATION SHARING: LEGAL CHALLENGES AND SOLUTIONS[*]

Andrew Nolan

SUMMARY

Over the course of the last year, a host of cyberattacks has been perpetrated on a number of high profile American companies. The high profile cyberattacks of 2014 and early 2015 appear to be indicative of a broader trend: the frequency and ferocity of cyberattacks are increasing, posing grave threats to the national interests of the United States. While considerable debate exists with regard to the best strategies for protecting America's various cyber-systems and promoting cybersecurity, one point of general agreement amongst cyber-analysts is the perceived need for enhanced and timely exchange of cyber-threat intelligence both within the private sector and between the private sector and the government. Nonetheless, there are many reasons why entities may opt to not participate in a cyber-information sharing scheme, including the potential liability that could result from sharing internal cyber-threat information with other private companies or the government. More broadly, the legal issues surrounding cybersecurity information sharing— whether it be with regard to sharing between two private companies or the

[*] This is an edited, reformatted and augmented version of a Congressional Research Service publication, No. R43941, dated March 16, 2015.

dissemination of cyber-intelligence within the federal government—are complex and have few certain resolutions. In this vein, this report examines the various legal issues that arise with respect to the sharing of cybersecurity intelligence, with a special focus on two distinct concepts: (1) sharing of cyberinformation within the government's possession and (2) sharing of cyber-information within the possession of the private sector.

With regard to cyber-intelligence that is possessed by the federal government, the legal landscape is *relatively* clear: ample legal authority exists for the Department of Homeland Security (DHS) to serve as the central repository and distributor of cyber-intelligence for the federal government. Nonetheless, the legal authorities that do exist often overlap, perhaps resulting in confusion as to which of the multiple sub-agencies within DHS or even outside of DHS should be leading efforts on the distribution of cyber-information within the government and with the public. Moreover, while the government has wide authority to disclose cyber-intelligence within its possession, that authority is not limitless and is necessarily tied to laws that restrict the government's ability to release sensitive information within its possession.

With regard to cyber-intelligence that is possessed by the private sector, legal issues are clouded with uncertainty. A private entity that wishes to share cyber-intelligence with another company, an information sharing organization like an Information Sharing and Analysis Organization (ISAO) or an Information Sharing and Analysis Centers (ISAC), or the federal government may be exposed to civil or even criminal liability from a variety of different federal and state laws. Moreover, because of the uncertainty that pervades the interplay between laws of general applicability—like federal antitrust or privacy law—and their specific application to cyberintelligence sharing, it may be very difficult for any private entity to accurately assess potential liability that could arise by participating in a sharing scheme. In addition, concerns may arise with regard to how the government collects and maintains privately held cyber-intelligence, including fears that the information disclosed to the government could (1) be released through a public records request; (2) result in the forfeit of certain intellectual property rights; (3) be used against a private entity in a subsequent regulatory action; or (4) risk the privacy rights of individuals whose information may be encompassed in disclosed cyber-intelligence.

The report concludes by examining the major legislative proposal—including the Cyber Intelligence Sharing and Protection Act (CISPA), Cybersecurity Information Sharing Act (CISA), and the Cyber Threat Sharing Act (CTSA)—and the potential legal issues that such laws could prompt.

INTRODUCTION

Over the course of the last year, a host of cyberattacks[1] have been perpetrated on a number of high profile American companies. In January 2014, Target announced that hackers, using malware,[2] had digitally impersonated one of the retail giant's contractors,[3] stealing vast amounts of data—including the names, mailing addresses, phone numbers or email addresses for up to 70 million individuals and the credit card information of 40 million shoppers.[4] Cyberattacks in February and March of 2014 potentially exposed contact and log-in information of eBay's customers, prompting the online retailer to ask its more than 200 million users to change their passwords.[5] In September, it was revealed that over the course of five months cyber-criminals tried to steal the credit card information of more than fifty million shoppers of the world's largest home improvement retailer, Home Depot.[6] One month later, J.P. Morgan Chase, the largest U.S. bank by assets, disclosed that contact information for about 76 million households was captured in a cyberattack earlier in the year.[7] In perhaps the most infamous cyberattack of 2014, in late November, Sony Pictures Entertainment suffered a "significant system disruption" as a result of a "brazen cyber attack"[8] that resulted in the leaking of the personal details of thousands of Sony employees.[9] And in February of 2015, the health care provider Anthem Blue Cross Blue Shield disclosed that a "very sophisticated attack" obtained personal information relating to the company's customers and employees.[10]

The high profile cyberattacks of 2014 and early 2015 appear to be indicative of a broader trend: the frequency and ferocity of cyberattacks are increasing,[11] posing grave threats to the national interests of the United States. Indeed, the attacks on Target, eBay, Home Depot, J.P. Morgan-Chase, Sony Pictures, and Anthem were only a few of the many publicly disclosed cyberattacks perpetrated in 2014 and 2105.[12] Experts suggest that hundreds of thousands of other entities may have suffered similar incidents during the same period,[13] with one survey indicating that 43% of firms in the United States had experienced a data breach in the past year.[14] Moreover, just as the cyberattacks of 2013—which included incidents involving companies like the *New York Times,* Facebook, Twitter, Apple, and Microsoft[15]—were eclipsed by those that occurred in 2014,[16] the consensus view is that 2015 and beyond will witness more frequent and more sophisticated cyber incidents.[17] To the extent that its expected rise outpaces any corresponding rise in the ability to defend against such attacks, the result could be troubling news for countless businesses that rely more and more on computers in all aspects of their operations, as the economic losses resulting from a single cyberattack can be extremely costly.[18] And the resulting effects of a cyberattack can have effects beyond a single company's bottom line. As "nations are becoming ever more dependent on information and information technology,"[19] the threat posed by any one cyberattack can have "devastating collateral and cascading effects across a wide range of physical, economic and social systems."[20] With reports that foreign nations—such as Russia, China, Iran, and North Korea –may be using cyberspace as a new front to wage war,[21] fears abound that a cyberattack could be used to shut down the nation's electrical grid,[22] hijack a commercial airliner,[23] or even launch a nuclear weapon with a single keystroke.[24] In short, the potential exists that the United States could suffer a "cyber Pearl Harbor," an attack that would "cause physical destruction and loss of life"[25] and expose—in the words of one prominent cybersecurity expert–"vulnerabilities of staggering proportions."[26]

Given the growing and potentially grave threat posed by cyberattacks, one of the stated priorities of the President and congressional leadership is to enact laws that ensure that both the public and private sector are prepared to meet the cyber-challenges of the future.[27] While considerable debate exists with regard to the best strategies and methods for protecting America's various cybersystems,[28] one point of "general agreement" amongst cyber-analysts is the perceived need for enhanced and timely exchange of cyber-threat intelligence[29] both within the private sector and between the private sector and the government.[30] The argument for the real time sharing of cyber-intelligence—which could include the sharing of vulnerability data (the vulnerabilities an intruder might exploit to gain access to a computer system), threat data (the types of malware circulating the Internet and the nature of the threats a given entity has faced), and countermeasure data (the steps an entity has taken to prevent or mitigate the effects of a cyberattack)[31]—is grounded in the idea that effective cybersecurity depends upon robust knowledge about potential threats and wide dissemination of the best practices and strategies to combat such threats.[32]

Despite widespread agreement about the need for enhanced cyber-information sharing, there is similar agreement among cyber-experts that current public and private sector information sharing efforts are simply inadequate.[33] While there may be many reasons why entities may opt to not participate in a cyber-information sharing scheme,[34] a primary rationale for such a decision concerns the potential *liability* that could result from sharing internal cyber-threat information with other private companies or the government. Indeed, in a recent survey of over 700 information technology security practitioners, half of the respondents listed worries about "potential liability [from] sharing" as the main reason for not participating in an initiative for exchanging threat information.[35] More broadly, the legal issues surrounding cybersecurity information sharing—whether it be with regard to sharing between two private companies or the dissemination of cyber-intelligence within the federal government—are complex and have few certain resolutions. In this vein, this report analyzes the major legal issues regarding cyber-threat information sharing by beginning with a discussion of the current legal authorities respecting the exchange of cyber-intelligence. Included in this discussion will be an examination of the various sources of liability that could result from information sharing. The report concludes by discussing several of the major legislative proposals aimed at reforming federal cyber-information sharing laws and potential legal issues that such laws could prompt.

CONCEPTUALIZING THE LEGAL ISSUES REGARDING CYBER INFORMATION SHARING

While often the concept of "cyber-information sharing" is thought of as a monolith, the sharing of cyber-intelligence touches on three related, but distinct concepts. First, cyber-information sharing is often used in the context of describing efforts to promote the dissemination of cyberintelligence *from* the federal government *to* other government entities or the private sector. This sort of cyber information sharing would occur, for example, when the Federal Bureau of Investigation (FBI) provides the Department of Homeland Security (DHS) or privately owned banks with the IP addresses of computers known to have launched distributed denial of service (DDoS) attacks against other entities within the financial sector.[36] Second, cyber-threat information sharing also embraces the concept of private entities sharing cyber-intelligence with each other, such as when several companies in a particular sector establish a formal exchange or formal agreements to share relevant cyber-information with each other.[37] Finally, cyberinformation sharing also describes when *private* entities share cyber-threat information in their possession *with* the government. Such information sharing could occur, for example, when private security firms report to DHS details about potential cyber-vulnerabilities unearthed in research.[38] While collectively these three variants on the concept of cyber-information sharing have some commonalities, each also raises separate legal challenges that may impede cyberintelligence dissemination more generally.

SHARING CYBER-INFORMATION IN THE POSSESSION OF THE GOVERNMENT

Perhaps the area in which there is the most legal clarity with respect to cyber-information sharing pertains to the authority of the federal government – and its subcomponents—to disseminate cyber threat information within the government and with the private sector. Two central components of DHS lead efforts to distribute cyber-intelligence to others in the government[39] and the private sector.[40]

First, the **Office of Intelligence and Analysis** (I&A), an entity established under Section 201 of the Homeland Security Act of 2002 (Homeland Security Act or the Act),[41] is generally authorized to "access and receive" information and intelligence from "agencies of the Federal Government, State and local government agencies (including law enforcement agencies), and private sector entities"[42] in order to "identify and assess" "terrorist threats to the homeland" and "actual and potential vulnerabilities to the homeland."[43] In addition, the I&A is responsible for "integrat[ing] relevant information, analysis, and vulnerability assessments" and disseminating such information in "both classified and unclassified formats, as appropriate" to "other agencies of the Federal Government, State, and local government agencies and authorities, the private sector, and other entities."[44] In turn, pursuant to 6 U.S.C. Section 143, DHS, through I&A, is required to provide to state and localities "analysis and warnings related to threats to, and vulnerabilities of," "critical information systems,"[45] a term of art presumably[46] controlled by the Homeland Security Act's definition for the term "critical infrastructure":

> [S]ystems ... so vital to the United States that the incapacity or destruction of such systems ... would have a debilitating impact on security, national economic security, national public health or safety, or any combination of those matters.[47]

Moreover, DHS is authorized "upon request" to provide the same "analysis and warnings" to "private entities that own or operate critical information systems."[48] In practice, the I&A has primarily exercised its authority by focusing its efforts on *analyses* of cyber-threat information and the distribution of those analyses to various public and private entities.[49]

In addition to the I&A, DHS's **National Protection and Programs Directorate** (NPPD) and its subcomponents play perhaps an even more important role with respect to the sharing of cyberthreat information with other government and private entities.[50] Within the NPPD exists the Office of Cybersecurity and Communications (CS&C), an office Congress created in 2006[51] that is tasked with overseeing the "security, resiliency, and reliability of the nation's cyber and communications infrastructure."[52] To execute this mission, CS&C, supports "24x7 information sharing, analysis, and incident response" through the National Cybersecurity and Communication Integration Center (NCCIC or Center).[53] Established in 2009, the NCCIC is a "24-hour, DHS-led coordinated watch and warning center" monitoring "threats and incidents affecting the nation's critical information technology and cyber infrastructure."[54] NCCIC, through the United States Computer Emergency Readiness Team (US-CERT), helps operate "key aspects" of several information sharing programs, including the Cyber Information Sharing and Collaboration Program (CISCP) and Enhanced Cybersecurity Services (ECS).[55] CISCP allows for often *unclassified*[56] "cyber threat, incident, and vulnerability information" to be disclosed "in near real-time" with private information sharing organizations and select owners and operators of so-called critical infrastructure and key resources.[57] ECS entails a "voluntary information sharing program" that, in part, "shares *sensitive and classified* government ... cyber threat information" with certain private actors.[58]

In late 2014, Congress enacted the National Cybersecurity Protection Act of 2014 (NCPA), which formally codified NCCIC's authority, allowing the "Center to carry out certain responsibilities of the Under Secretary" for the NPPD.[59] Specifically, the NCPA confirmed that the NCCIC's functions include serving as an "interface" for the "real-time" "sharing of information related to cybersecurity risks, incidents, analysis, and warnings between Federal and non-Federal entities."[60] Furthermore, the NCPA directs the Center to provide a number of additional services, such as technical assistance, risk management support, and incident response capabilities to both public and private entities.[61] The NCPA requires NCCIC to include representatives of federal agencies, state and local governments, and private sector owners and operators of critical information systems,[62] while still providing the Under Secretary for the NPPD with discretion with respect to the precise makeup of the Center.[63] In February of 2015, in keeping with NCCIC's statutory role, President Obama, in an Executive Order, mandated that the Center "engage in continuous, collaborative, and inclusive coordination with" Information Sharing and Analysis Organizations (ISAOs),[64] a formal or informal entity or collaboration created or employed by public or private sector organizations that gather, analyze, and disseminate cyber-threat information.[65]

The Homeland Security Act, as amended by the NCPA, provides significant authority for DHS to disseminate a wide range of cyber-threat intelligence within the possession of the federal government to other government agencies and to the private sector. Earlier iterations of the Homeland Security Act seemingly cabined DHS's authority to collect and share cyberintelligence only to the extent such information respected a "terrorist threat"[66] or would pertain to "critical information systems."[67] In contrast, the NCPA provides NCCIC the authority to share cyber-information to the extent that such information relates to "cybersecurity risks,"[68] a term of art that encompasses any "threats" and "vulnerabilities" to information systems and "any related consequences caused by or resulting" from a host of actions that could compromise an information system or the information stored on an information system.[69] In other words, given DHS's discretion in designating various entities to participate in the NCCIC,[70] it appears DHS has fairly broad authority to disseminate federal cyber threat information throughout the private sector, regardless of whether the information pertains to an industry that is "so vital to the United States that the incapacity or destruction" of that industry's assets or information systems would be "debilitating" to the country.[71] In fact, one issue that has been raised by commentators is whether the statutory authority allotted to the various entities within DHS—such as I&A and NPPD—to engage in cyber-information sharing is so broad and ill-defined that confusion could result internally within the Department as to who the central actor should be with respect to the sharing of federal cyber-intelligence.[72] The same argument could plausibly be made with respect to the authority to disseminate cyber-intelligence amongst the various entities of the federal government, as entities like the I&A[73] and NPPD[74] within DHS and new entities outside of DHS, like the newly formed Cyber Threat Intelligence Integration Center (CTICC)[75] appear to possess overlapping legal authorities with respect to the internal sharing of cyber-information within the federal government.[76]

Nonetheless, DHS's ability to share federal cyber-intelligence is not limitless. First, cyber-threat information the government provides to the private sector generally must occur on a voluntary basis.[77] The plain language of Section 223 of the Homeland Security Act limits DHS's ability to share cyber-intelligence with "private entities that own or operate critical information systems," such that information sharing can only occur "upon [those entities'] request."[78] And indeed, the NCPA contains an even more explicit provision disclaiming the Act from being "construed to require any private entity" to request any assistance from the Secretary of DHS.[79] In other words, under current law, DHS generally does not have the authority to "mandate private sector participation" in federal cyber information sharing efforts,[80] leading some to question the value of the current voluntary information sharing scheme.[81]

Second, other laws outside of the context of cybersecurity may limit the ability of the government to disseminate cyber-threat information. The Homeland Security Act itself requires DHS to ensure that any intelligence in its possession "is protected from unauthorized disclosure and handled and used only for the performance of official duties."[82] More specifically, the Act mandates that DHS adhere to (1) the requirements of the National Security Act of 1947 to the extent any information pertains to intelligence sources and methods and (2) any authorities of the Attorney General "concerning sensitive law enforcement information."[83] In other words, to the extent any federal cyber-intelligence contains sensitive information, such as the sources or methods that are the heart of an ongoing cybercrime investigation,[84] the government may be limited in its ability to disclose such information.

Beyond laws aimed at limiting disclosures that may inhibit core governmental functions, laws aimed at preserving privacy and civil liberties may also restrict DHS's ability to share certain cyber-information. The Homeland Security Act requires DHS to "ensure ... that any information databases and analytical tools developed and utilized by the Department"—which would presumably include programs like CISCP and ECS—"treat information in such databases in a manner that complies with applicable Federal law on privacy."[85] Moreover, the NCPA requires that the NCCIC "comply with all policies, regulations, and laws that protect the privacy and civil liberties of United States persons."[86] As such, if DHS's cyber intelligence included, for example, individually identifiable information—like a name or a social security number—laws like the Privacy Act of 1974 may restrict the manner in which the government may disclose such information in a cyber-information sharing program.[87]

Collectively, the legal effect of the various federal disclosure and privacy laws may limit the efficacy of any cyber-information DHS provides private entities. As one commentator recently noted, the resulting "sanitation" of cyber-intelligence has a dual effect.[88] First, the host of federal agencies that "own classified or law enforcement information germane to a particular warning" "must be coordinated with as part of the review process," resulting in significant delays before DHS can release any information to a private entity, by which time the information may be irrelevant.[89] Second, even if DHS releases government cyber threat information in a timely manner, the cyber intelligence resulting after agency review of the underlying material may omit critical information that is "actually useful to industry."[90]

SHARING CYBER-INFORMATION IN THE POSSESSION OF PRIVATE ENTITIES

Whereas the law governing the dissemination of cyber-threat information in the possession of the federal government is relatively straightforward, the legal landscape surrounding the sharing of cyber-intelligence that is in the possession of private parties stands in stark contrast. Indeed, there is an array of legal concerns—some more theoretical than actual—that shroud the law governing the sharing of privately-held cyber-threat information in a cloud of uncertainty and create disincentives against the sharing of such information by private parties.[91] The legal issues can be divided between those that arise when private companies share cyber-information with each other and those that occur when private companies share cyber-intelligence with the government.

Sharing Cyber-Information with Another Private Entity

Information security professionals within the private sector have "long relied" on information from other private entities to "gain insight into cybersecurity threats and vulnerabilities."[92] And often the most valuable cyber-intelligence comes from peers in other companies, including direct competitors that may be subject to similar cybercrimes.[93] Private cyber-information sharing can take many forms, from informal arrangements, such as peer discussions via phone, email, or in person, to formal sharing arrangements, such as cyber-intelligence sharing through an Information Sharing and Analysis Center (ISAC), a private sector nonprofit corporation formed to facilitate the sharing of information on cyber-threats, incidents and vulnerabilities among members within a particular sector.[94] At times, the federal government has been quite supportive of such private efforts to share cyber-intelligence. Indeed, the impetus for ISACs was Presidential Decision

Directive-63, issued by President Clinton in 1998, which initially called for the creation of industry-specific ISACs.[95] Nonetheless, there are several bodies of law whose basic norms run counter to the concept of a private business sharing cyber-threat information with an industry peer, raising potential liability issues for those in the private sector that wish to exchange cyberintelligence.[96] Without any overarching federal law governing private exchanges of cyber-threat information, the potential remains for various laws facially unrelated to cyber-information sharing to discourage such activity within the private sector.

Privacy Laws

A variety of state and federal privacy laws govern the collection, storage, use, and dissemination of electronic information, potentially leaving limited room for cyber-intelligence sharing amongst private actors or between private actors and the government.

The most pertinent *federal* privacy law is the Electronic Communications Privacy Act of 1986 (ECPA), which contains three titles: (1) Title I, the Wiretap Act,[97] which regulates the interception of communications content in transit; (2) Title II, the Stored Wire and Electronic Communications and Transactional Records Access Act[98] (Stored Communications Act or SCA), which governs electronic communications already transmitted and currently in storage; and (3) Title III, the Pen Register and Trap and Traces Devices Act (Pen/Trap Act),[99] which regulates the interception of noncontent communications, such as phone numbers or IP addresses. Each section of ECPA is potentially relevant to those private entities considering sharing cyber-intelligence information.

The Wiretap Act

The Wiretap Act generally provides for criminal[100] and civil damages[101] against anyone who "intentionally intercepts, endeavors to intercept, or procures any other person to intercept or endeavor to intercept" any covered communication,[102] which includes electronic communication.[103] To "intercept" an electronic communication is to use "any electronic, mechanical, or other device" to acquire the "contents" or the "substance, purport, or meaning" of the communication,[104] contemporaneously with the transmission.[105] Relatedly, the statute also generally prohibits a "person or entity providing electronic communication service to the public" from intentionally divulging the contents of any electronic communication while in transmission other than to the "addressee or intended recipient of such communication."[106] Perhaps most relevant to cyber-information *sharing*, the Wiretap Act also prohibits the *disclosure or use* of the contents of any electronic communication that was obtained in violation of the statute, such an illegal interception of electronic communications.[107]

Putting to the side the several exceptions contained in the Wiretap Act, on its face, ECPA's general prohibition on the interception of electronic communications would appear to encompass any strategy for detecting cyber-threats that involved scanning the *contents* of an electronic communication while in transmission,[108] and ECPA's general prohibition on an electronic service provider divulging the *contents* of any communication while in transmission may bar the *real time* transmission of certain cyber-intelligence.[109] While cyber-intelligence may often not include the contents of an electronic communication and may merely contain, for example, the IP address of the origin of malware, as one commentator has suggested, many common cyber-threat detection methods require using the contents of electronic communications—such as text within the body of an email—to determine whether a particular communication is malicious.[110] Moreover, to be effective, cyber-information sharing often necessitates the use of real time sharing of cyber-threat information.[111] Nonetheless, the Wiretap Act contains two key exceptions to its general prohibition that may limit the scope of the law as it pertains to cyber-information collection and sharing.[112]

First, the Wiretap Act includes an exception to its general prohibitions when there is the presence of consent to the otherwise illicit interception or disclosure ("consent exception").[113] A private actor can only rely on the consent exception where one of the parties to the communication has given prior consent to the interception or divulgence.[114] Courts reviewing the question of whether a party to the communication consented to an interception or disclosure will look into the "dimensions of the consent" and then ascertain whether the act in question "exceeded those boundaries."[115]

With respect to a private entity's efforts to collect content-based cyber-threat information and disseminate such information, the Wiretap Act's consent exception, while often a viable route to avoid liability, raises several difficult legal questions. For example, determining who is a "party to the communication" when someone is launching a cyberattack can be very difficult, as the cybercriminal may be using multiple computers and the ultimate destination of the hacker's communication may be unclear.[116] While an entity attempting to monitor its system for cyberintruders could argue that it is a party to the underlying electronic communication being monitored because the data is flowing on its network and is being directed toward its computers and employees,[117] such an interpretation of what it means to be a party to a communication may eliminate any privacy protections for the individuals who are directly participating in the electronic communication.[118] Instead, a court may likely interpret that a party to a communication must be the individuals who actually take part in the electronic conversation.[119]

Moreover, assuming that the private entity acquiring cyber-threat information is not a party to the communication, consent must be obtained from one of the individuals taking part in the communication, which, in turn, depends on the dimensions of the consent and whether the interception or divulgence of the contents of electronic communication exceeded the boundaries of the consent.[120] Such an inquiry can be quite context specific,[121] inviting litigation and creating legal uncertainty for entities wishing to engage in cyber-information sharing. For example, courts have come to differing conclusions as to whether an electronic communications service provider's customer has consented to having the provider intercept certain communications, largely because of the specific nature of the interception in question and the precise terms of service to which the customer agreed.[122] Importantly, consent cannot be "casually" inferred,[123] and absent actual notice of the nature of the interception or divulgence, consent can only be implied if the "surrounding circumstances convincingly show that the party knew about and consented to the interception."[124] Courts, interpreting the consent exception narrowly to ensure the exemption does not swallow the rule, have held that merely providing a person notice that an entity has the capability of intercepting communications cannot be considered implied consent.[125] And deficient notice will "almost always defeat a claim of consent."[126] As a consequence, for a private entity that wishes to employ and share the results of a cyber-threat detector, which often is created with the goal of invisibly tracking communications without alerting either internal or external users of its operation, notice to a party of an electronic communication that is sufficient to create consent may, at times, defeat the entire purpose of monitoring and sharing the contents of electronic communications.

Second, the Wiretap Act also includes a "provider exception" which allows the provider of electronic communications to "intercept, disclose, or use" the contents of communications when the activity is a "necessary incident to ... the protection of the rights or property of the provider of that service."[127] On its face, the provider exception is limited to protecting the "rights or property of the provider," as opposed to any third party.[128] While at least one court has read the provider exception broadly to allow a service provider to intercept or disclose covered communications for purposes of aiding third parties,[129] several courts have cabined the provider exception in terms of whether the interception was done for the purpose of protecting the provider's own "equipment and rights."[130] And the Department of Justice's (DOJ's) Office of Legal Counsel has likewise concluded that the provider exception "must protect the provider's own rights or property, and not those of any third party.... "[131] As a consequence, there is a strong argument that while ECPA may authorize private entities to monitor their *own* system and to share cyber-intelligence necessary to protect their *own* system,[132] the law likely does not authorize service providers to disclose or divulge in real time to other private entities or the government[133] the contents of electronic communications for the purpose of protecting a third party's property or rights.[134] In other words, a more narrow reading of the provider exception may cast doubt on the legality of certain cyberinformation sharing methods.

The Stored Communications Act

In contrast to the Wiretap Act, which focuses on the interception and disclosure of the contents of communications in transmission, Title II of ECPA—the SCA—is centrally concerned with access to and the disclosure of both content and *non-content* based electronic communications that are kept in *storage*.[135] In relevant part,[136] the SCA in Section 2702 *generally* prohibits service providers engaged in either "electronic communications service" (ECS) or remote computing service (RCS) to the public from divulging the contents[137] of communications in their possessions[138] and subjects those that violate the SCA to civil liability.[139] Notwithstanding that general statement about Section 2702, the SCA is a notoriously complicated statute,[140] and, accordingly, Section 2702(a)'s central prohibition regarding the disclosure of the contents of communications requires some clarification and several caveats.

First, to run afoul of Section 2702(a)(1)-(2)'s prohibition, the entity in question must provide *either* ECS or RCS. ECS, as defined under the SCA, includes any service which provides users the means to "send or receive ... electronic communication,"[141] such as businesses that provide text messaging[142] or email[143] services. An RCS, as defined by the SCA , entails "the provisions to the public of computer storage or processing services by means of an electronic communications system."[144] Courts have interpreted an RCS to refer to the long-term processing or storage of data by an off-site third party.[145] Second, not all disclosures by an ECS or RCS are prohibited by the SCA; only disclosures of the *contents* of communications[146]—as opposed to address information, like an email address[147]—would fall within the prohibition. Third, for an *ECS provider*, only disclosures made while the underlying communication is *in electronic storage* amount to a violation of the statute[148]—a status defined by the act as either (1) temporary, intermediate storage of an electronic communication incidental to the transmission of that communication; or (2) any storage of an electronic communication for backup protection.[149] The definition of "electronic storage" has been the source of considerable disagreement, with one prominent judicial opinion interpreting "electronic storage" to encompass both electronic messages that have yet to be delivered to their intended recipient, as well as electronic messages in backup storage by the provider until "the underlying message has expired in the normal course,"[150] while others have criticized the notion of "electronic storage" encompassing opened emails serviced by an ECS.[151] Fourth, for an *RCS provider* to violate 18 U.S.C. Section 2702(a)(2), the provider must disclose the contents of communications that are (1) "on behalf of, and received by" a subscriber or customer of the service; and (2) "solely for the purpose of providing storage or computer processing services to ... [that] subscriber or customer."[152] The statutory prohibition necessarily excludes providers of RCS to the public who are authorized to access the contents of communication for purposes other than for storage and computer processing, such as for advertising purposes.[153]

Putting to the side the exceptions to SCA's prohibition found in 18 U.S.C. Section 2702(a)(1)-(2), unlike the Wiretap Act, the SCA's prohibition on disclosing communications in storage will be unlikely to prohibit many forms of cyber-information sharing. After all, to violate the statute, a company must not only disclose the *contents* of communications to another private entity, but the company doing the disclosure must provide ECS or RCS to the *public*.[154] In other words, if, for example, an email provider to the public shares the IP address that was the source of a malicious email to a ISAO, that email provider did not share content information and therefore likely did not violate the SCA. Moreover, if a private entity provides email services to its employees and shares the text of an email that is the source of a computer virus with another company, that private entity likely did not violate the SCA because that entity does not provide ECS or RCS to the *public*.

Nonetheless, many Internet Service Providers (ISPs) or email providers ostensibly provide ECS or RCS to the public,[155] and those companies may be interested in sharing the *contents* of information with outsiders for cybersecurity purposes. If so, it is uncontroversial to say that because of disputes over key terms like "electronic storage" and "RCS" and "ECS," the SCA, as currently written and interpreted, is hardly a model of clarity.[156] The resulting ambiguity about the legality of information sharing within the SCA's general ambit may deter providers of ECS or RCS to the public from sharing cyber-threat information with other private entities.[157] After all, ambiguity in the law often breeds litigation, and the costs of litigation may be significant enough to deter companies from engaging in cyber-information sharing.[158]

The hesitancy to participate in information sharing schemes may exist notwithstanding several exceptions[159] to the SCA's general prohibition on the disclosure of certain types of electronic communication held in storage.[160] For example, while the SCA excludes from its prohibition on the disclosure of communications disclosures made to a "person employed or authorized ... to forward such communication to its destination,"[161] that exception only eliminates liability for those entities wishing to gather and share cyber-threat information *within* that organization[162] and does not sanction the sharing of the contents of a communication with an outsider. Moreover, the SCA also contains a consent exception, allowing an ECS or RCS provider to divulge the contents of a communication if the sender or recipient of that communication consents or, in the case of an RCS, if the *subscriber* of the communication consents to the disclosure.[163] Like the Wiretap Act's consent exception, the SCA's consent exception is largely fact dependent, arguably providing little assurance to a communications services provider that wishes to wholly eliminate litigation risk.[164] More specifically, the scope of the SCA's consent exception is directly linked to a service provider's status as providing ECS or RCS, which may make the viability of the consent defense contingent on the murky distinction between when a provider is acting in either role.[165] Finally, similar to the Wiretap Act, the SCA also contains a provider exception, and, much like its counterpart in the Wiretap Act, the SCA's provider exception is limited to allowing disclosures that are necessary for the "protection of the rights or property of the *provider*"[166] and arguably does not extend to the protection of third parties that the provider may wish to share cyber-intelligence.[167]

The Pen/Trap Act

The final major federal privacy law potentially relevant to cyber-information sharing amongst private parties is found in Title III of ECPA, Pen/Trap Act.[168] The Pen/Trap Act has been referred to as the "non-content counterpart" to the Wiretap Act, in that the Pen/Trap Act is concerned with the *real time* capturing of *non-content* information,[169] such as IP addresses and the "to" and "from" fields in an email.[170] Specifically, in 18 U.S.C. Section 3121, the Pen/Trap Act generally prohibits any person from installing or using a "pen register or a trap and trace device," devices used outside of the ordinary course of business that capture either incoming or outgoing non-content electronic information about the source of a communication, without first receiving permission from a court.[171] Violations of the Pen/Trap Act can result in criminal penalties, including not more than one year in prison.[172] Like its counterpart the Wiretap Act, the Pen/Trap Act, also contains several exceptions to its general prohibition, including a (1) "provider exception," which permits service providers to use pen/trap devices for the "operation, maintenance, and testing of [an] ... electronic communication service" or to protect the "rights and property" of the provider or the "users of that service from abuse of service or unlawful use of service,"[173] (2) "consent exception," which allows the use of pen/trap devices where the user of the service has provided consent.[174] Nonetheless, in sharp contrast to the Wiretap Act and the SCA, the Pen/Trap Act contains no provisions barring the *disclosure or divulgence* of non-content information derived from a pen/trap device.[175]

For a private entity wishing to share non-content cyber-threat information with a third party, the Pen/Trap Act likely does not raise serious legal concerns. First, the Pen/Trap statute's provider exception likely eliminates any potential criminal liability that could arise from a company monitoring and capturing non-content information for cybersecurity purposes. After all, the Pen/Trap Act's provider exception sweeps more broadly than the provider exceptions in the Wiretap Act or the SCA, in that Title III of ECPA allows providers to use a pen/trap device "relating to the operation, maintenance, and testing of [an] ... electronic communication system.... "[176] Given that nearly any electronic communication system, such as email or Internet communication, necessarily depends on routing information from one source to another,[177] it is arguable that most private entities with genuine cybersecurity concerns may likely be capturing non-content information as a natural product of the operating of an electronic communication system anyway.[178]

Moreover, even if an entity's decision to capture non-content address information is not related to the "operation, maintenance, and testing of [an] ... electronic communication system," the second clause of the Pen/Trap Act's provider exception allows the use of a pen/trap device to protect the rights or property of the provider or the users of the service from "abuse of service or unlawful use of service,"[179] which would appear to encompass the circumstance where a private entity collects non-content information to identify the source of a potential cyber-threat.[180] In addition, even if the provider exception does not allow the use of a pen/trap device, the consent exception would allow a provider to capture non-content cyber-threat information with the agreement of the provider's user.[181] Importantly, because the Pen/Trap Act only criminalizes the illegal use of pen/trap devices and does not regulate the disclosures of non-content information culled from a pen/trap device, once a provider has legally used a pen/trap device, there appears to be no reason why a private entity should fear liability under the Pen/Trap Act if a company were, for example, to share the IP address that was the source of malware with another private company.[182]

Other Federal and State Privacy Laws

While ECPA is the most prominently mentioned federal privacy law that could implicate cyberthreat information sharing efforts, other federal privacy laws could also plausibly deter the exchange of cyber-intelligence amongst private entities. As noted above, ECPA's privacy protections are tied to (1) the age of the underlying communication, with communications in storage generally getting less protection than communications that are being transferred in real time, and (2) whether the underlying communication reveals substantive content, with non-content information, such as IP addresses and email addresses, receiving fewer protections under the statute.[183] In contrast to ECPA, a host of various federal privacy laws target *specific industries* that tend to control *personally identifying information* (PII), such as names, addresses, phone numbers, or Social Security numbers. For example, the Cable Communications Policy Act of 1984 (CCPA) generally prohibits "cable operators"[184] from collecting and disclosing PII,[185] subjecting entities that violate the CCPA's privacy protections to civil liability.[186] Some courts, interpreting the CCPA, have concluded that cable providers when providing Internet services can be subject to the Act's privacy provisions,[187] raising the specter of civil liability if a cable ISP were to disclose PII—like a name or an email address—while sharing cyber-threat information with another private entity.

Much as the CCPA could raise liability concerns for cable ISPs wishing to share cyberinformation with other private entities, so too could a variety of federal privacy laws raise legal questions for the entities that are regulated by such laws. Indeed, several discrete federal privacy laws regulate how PII is collected and disseminated. These laws target a variety of distinct entities, including

- consumer reporting agencies[188]
- operators of websites or online services directed to children[189]
- financial institutions[190]

- videotape service providers[191]
- educational agencies or institutions[192]
- health plans, health care clearinghouses, and health care providers[193]
- telecommunications carriers[194]

To the extent any one of these entities wishes to share cyber-intelligence within its possession with others in the private sector, legal questions may abound if any of the information to be shared contains material that is potentially protected under federal privacy law. None of the aforementioned federal privacy laws specifically contemplate any exceptions for the sharing of cyber-information for cybersecurity purposes. And, there is very little, if any, case law examining how a given law applies to the specific context of the collection and dissemination of information for cybersecurity purposes, leaving a legal lacuna for those regulated entities that may wish to engage in cyber-information sharing.

Beyond *federal* privacy laws, *states and localities* have enacted countless laws that may prevent or deter private entities from sharing cyber-intelligence with others. All but one of the fifty states has an eavesdropping law that is generally modeled off the Wiretap Act,[195] and a majority of states regulate the collection and dissemination of electronic communications.[196] While many of the state communications privacy laws mirror federal law, state laws are often more restrictive or may simply regulate different aspects of communications privacy than federal law,[197] multiplying the legal questions facing those entities wishing to engage in cyber-information sharing. For example, eight states currently generally require both parties to an electronic communication to consent to its interception and/or further dissemination,[198] allowing, in the words of one commentator, cyber "attackers a veto on whether their packets are inspected for malicious code"[199] and potentially deterring some entities from collecting and divulging cyber-threat information to others.

Moreover, much like the federal government, some states have laws that target the collection and divulgence of PII within the possession of entities that may wish to engage in cyber-information sharing.[200] Although an examination of the various state privacy laws is beyond the scope of this report, these laws may raise liability concerns for entities that do business in multiple states and wish to disseminate cyber-threat information outside of the company.

Antitrust Laws

In addition to federal and state privacy laws, antitrust laws also have generated liability concerns for private entities that wish to collaborate over cybersecurity.[201] Indeed, in a recent survey, more than a quarter of IT professionals identified "anti-competitive concerns" as one of the central reasons for not participating in information sharing programs.[202] Deterring anticompetitive conduct by businesses, such as coordinated action that undermines competition, is at the heart of federal antitrust law.[203] Specifically, the Supreme Court in interpreting the Sherman Antitrust Act—the "primary federal antitrust enforcement mechanism"[204]—has recognized that the law's facial prohibition in Section 1 on *all* contracts, combinations, or conspiracies that result in a restraint of trade or commerce[205] should be read to prohibit only those agreements that *unreasonably* restrain trade.[206] While courts interpreting the reach of the Sherman Act generally view any concerted activity with some degree of skepticism,[207] certain agreements, such as price fixing and market allocation among competitors, are viewed as being so "inherently anticompetitive that each is illegal *per se* without inquiry into the harm it has actually caused."[208] Other agreements, such as mergers or joint ventures that may facilitate more effective competition, are adjudged under the "rule of reason," in which a court will weigh the legitimate justifications for a restraint against any anticompetitive effects.[209] In other words, determining whether a given agreement between two private businesses violates the Sherman Act largely depends upon the specifics of that particular agreement.[210] Businesses that are alleged to violate federal antitrust laws face potential criminal prosecutions,[211] as well as civil actions that could be initiated by the federal government,[212] state governments,[213] or even aggrieved private litigants.[214] Civil litigation risks treble damages—damages three times the amount of actual damage—being paid to successful plaintiffs.[215]

While fears abound that any coordination on cyber-defense could give rise to antitrust liability,[216] the likelihood of such liability will likely depend on the nature and purpose of the underlying agreement to share cyber-threat information.[217] Exchanges of information among competitors do not constitute *per se* violations of the Sherman Act, as the Supreme Court has found that such practices can "increase economic efficiency and render markets more ... competitive."[218] Moreover, the Court has been reluctant "to condemn rules adopted by professional associations as unreasonable *per se*.... "[219] As a consequence, perhaps a few agreements to coordinate on cyberdefense—such as an agreement amongst competitors to "implement a uniform set of cyber-security practices"[220] by either agreeing to "pass on" certain associated costs to customers[221] or adopt cybersecurity practices that provide inferior products to end users[222]—may "amount to a 'naked' restraint that results in reflexive condemnation under the *per se* rule."[223] Nonetheless, most efforts to share cybersecurity information amongst private entities, particularly within a formal organization like an ISAC, will likely be adjudged under the rule of reason.[224] A rule of reason analysis would weigh the legitimate justifications for engaging in concerted efforts to share cyber-information against any anticompetitive effects.[225] As such, a rule of reason analysis regarding cyber-information sharing may weigh the interest in combatting fraudulent cyber-activity[226] versus the potentiality of certain actors being excluded from the cyber information forum for anticompetitive reasons.[227] Nonetheless, there is no case law that squarely addresses how antitrust laws apply to coordinated efforts to combat cyber-threats, and given the central role of common law in defining the limits of federal antitrust law, the net result may be considerable legal uncertainty for those private entities that may wish to engage in such activities.

Recognizing the legal uncertainty that exists with respect to antitrust law and cybersecurity information sharing, in April of 2014, DOJ and the Federal Trade Commission (FTC) issued a joint policy statement that attempted to clarify the extent to which the exchange of cyber-threat information amongst private parties could raise antitrust issues.[228] The joint policy statement confirmed that information sharing agreements are typically examined under a rule of reason analysis,[229] and the statement continued by recognizing that the exchange of cyber-threat information has numerous positive effects that will weigh in favor of its legality, including helping "secure our nation's networks of information and resources."[230] Moreover, the joint policy statement emphasized that the typical nature of cyber-threat information—described as being "very technical in nature"—is often unlikely to contain "competitively sensitive information" that would allow participants to "raise prices or reduce output, quality, service, or innovation."[231] Instead, the two agencies underscored that the primary antitrust concern in the context of cyber information sharing is the sharing competitively sensitive information, such as "current, and future prices, cost data, or output levels" that could allow for "competitive coordination among competitors."[232]

Notwithstanding the value of the joint guidance, as the guidance concedes, any analysis of the legality of a cyber-information sharing agreement is "intensely fact-driven,"[233] and, given the predominant role of the rule of reason with respect to examining the legality of any cyber-threat sharing agreements,[234] definitive conclusions by the government about the legality of cybersecurity information sharing arrangements vis-à-vis antitrust law may simply be impossible.[235] Moreover, given the role of private parties in enforcing federal antitrust law through civil lawsuits,[236] even if government entities like the FTC and the DOJ generally agreed that antitrust laws should not be enforced with respect to concerted actions over cybersecurity, nothing prevents an aggrieved private party from initiating an antitrust lawsuit to prevent collaboration over cyber-information sharing,[237] meaning that without a change in the current law liability risks from antitrust suits may remain for any private entity interested in sharing cybersecurity information.

Tort Law

Another often-cited source of liability that may dissuade private entities from participating in cyber-information sharing schemes is tort law, specifically torts founded upon negligence– that is, the fear that by sharing and obtaining cyber-information a private entity may be liable for negligently failing to act upon certain threat information.[238] Generally under tort law, to establish that a defendant has acted negligently, a plaintiff must show: (1) a duty of care owed to the plaintiff by the defendant; (2) a breach of that duty by the defendant; (3) causation (i.e., the resulting injury was both the "but for" and "proximate cause or foreseeable consequence of the risk created by the defendant's act or omission"); and (4) a cognizable injury or harm to the plaintiff.[239] In the context of a lawsuit following a cyberattack, an injured party may seek compensation from a company whose network was breached, arguing that the company owed its customers a duty of reasonable security to protect against cybercriminals stealing their data.[240] However, while courts have *generally* recognized that "cyber attacks are [a] foreseeable" risk for which a service provider must account,[241] courts have been fairly reluctant to find that a *particular* cyberattack should have been anticipated by a service provider.[242] After all, just as a business has no duty to protect its customers against unforeseeable crimes from third parties,[243] so too must the "duty to implement security thwarting third-party cybercrimes ... turn on whether the crime was foreseeable."[244] In other words, under tort law, a business likely does not have a duty to guard against "innovative [cyber-]breaches that have no known or effective defense at the time of the attack."[245]

Because tort liability for a cyberattack will likely turn on the amount of knowledge a given party may have about a cyberattack, cyber-information sharing schemes have the potential to change the tort liability calculus for those entities that participate. For example, if a company opts to *share* information about the origins of a recent cyberattack perpetrated on that company with a public information sharing group, like an ISAC, the company may be admitting that it could have foreseen the attack or mitigated its effects in some way, providing potential plaintiffs with credible evidence to support a potential tort lawsuit. Likewise, entities that *receive* information about a potential cyberattack, fail to act, and then subsequently are targeted by the attack, can no longer credibly claim that the harm from the cyberattack was unforeseeable. In this sense, tort law can have the perverse effect of incentivizing private entities to "simply stay[] in the dark" about potential cyberattacks and to not participate in cyber-information sharing programs.[246]

Nonetheless, even if participation in a cyber-information sharing agreement increases tort liability risks, it remains very difficult for a plaintiff to succeed on the theory that a private entity failed to prevent a cyberattack. First, in order for cyber-threat sharing to increase tort liability risks, an entity would have to have some considerable bad luck. The company in question would not only have to suffer a cyberattack, but that cyberattack would have to be linked to a cyberattack in which information was shared about, *and* the cyberattack would have to result in actual damages for a plaintiff. Notwithstanding popular media accounts regarding potential losses created by a cyberattack,[247] most of the cost of a cyberattack will be borne by the company attacked and will not result in actual losses for potential plaintiffs in a tort lawsuit, like a customer.[248] And courts have been loath to allow a lawsuit to proceed based on the potential for future injury resulting from a cyberattack.[249] Second, and perhaps most importantly, the economic loss doctrine—which prohibits parties from recovering financial losses, absent injury to person or property, under tort law[250]—often prevents recovery in a lawsuit respecting a cyberattack because "[m]any of the harms that would result from a cyber-attack on, say, the power grid or the financial sector would be purely economic in nature."[251] And indeed, in recent tort lawsuits regarding cyberattacks, courts have dismissed tort claims at early stages of the litigation because of the economic loss doctrine.[252] In short, the litigation risks posed by tort lawsuits respecting a cyberattack may be fairly minimal regardless of whether an entity is involved in cybersecurity sharing.[253]

Other Sources of Liability

Beyond privacy, antitrust, and negligent tort law, several other laws could be the source of liability concerns for private entities that choose to share cyber-information with each other. For example, the 2013 Target data breach incident led to a shareholder derivative suit against Target's officers and board of directors, that alleged that those actors violated fiduciary obligations of trust, loyalty, good faith, and due care by failing to take adequate steps to prevent the cyberattack and by making inaccurate disclosures to their shareholders about the extent of the damage from the attack.[254] Shared cyber-information could be critical evidence in a similar suit. If, for example, a company that suffered a data breach like Target shared cyber-threat information with an ISAC prior to the attack, one could imagine such evidence being used in a similar shareholder lawsuit to establish that the company's officers had specific knowledge about the company's cybervulnerabilities or the extent of a cyber-attack on a given day.

And a shareholder derivative lawsuit is only one genre of litigation that could both result from a cyberattack *and* be aided by shared cyber-information.[255] For example, institutional customers who sue a bank in the wake of a cyberattack that has resulted in fraudulent wire transfers could be helped by evidence that a bank knew about particular risks posed by a cyberattack. The general framework governing the rights and obligations between a bank and customers respecting fraudulent wire transfers is found in Article 4A of the Uniform Commercial Code (UCC).[256] Article 4A generally requires banks to bear the risk if a third party steals a customer's identity, resulting in a fraudulent wire transfer.[257] Nonetheless, the UCC contains an exception whereby a customer will bear the risk of a fraudulent payment order if: (1) a bank and its customer agree to implement a security procedure designed to protect against fraud; (2) the security procedure that is implemented is a "commercially reasonable" method of providing security against unauthorized payment orders; and (3) the bank demonstrates that it accepted the payment order in good faith and in compliance with the security procedure.[258] While the question of whether a particular security procedure can be deemed "commercially reasonable" will likely depend on the specific facts surrounding a cyberattack and the procedures a bank had in place to prevent such a fraudulent transfer,[259] one critical factor may be a bank's prior awareness of the risks posed by a cyberattack.[260] In this vein, knowledge that a bank knew about a cybersecurity risk because of shared cyber intelligence could implicate that bank's liability with regard to a suit under the UCC.

More broadly, there are "a myriad of legal theories, including ... breach of express or implied contract, state deceptive trade practices act violations or state data breach notification violations" that could be the basis for a lawsuit against an entity that suffered a data breach.[261] Shared cyberinformation could be critical evidence that helps prove, for example, the timing of when a cyberattack occurred or the company's knowledge of the attack and the sufficiency of the company's cyber-defenses at the time of the breach,[262] which could result in private entities being less likely to share cyber-intelligence with any other entity or organization.

Sharing Cyber -Information with the Government

Just as private entities are increasingly recognizing the need to access cyber-intelligence gathered by their peers,[263] the federal government may need access to cyber-threat information in the possession of the private sector in order to make informed decisions about the government's and the nation's cybersecurity needs. As Lisa Monaco, the President's Homeland Security Advisor, recently noted, the "private sector has vital information we don't always see unless they share it with us."[264] Nonetheless, obtaining cyber-intelligence from the private sector can be difficult for the federal government. Putting aside the difficult issues that may arise when a private party affirmatively *refuses* to divulge cyber-intelligence within its possession to the federal government and the government is forced to obtain, for example, a warrant or a subpoena to access such information,[265] the federal government may not know that a private entity possesses certain cyberintelligence, and the only way the government can learn about a potential cyber-threat is by having the private party voluntarily share that information with the government. The voluntary disclosure of cyber-intelligence to the government may, however, be something private parties are reluctant to do because of various legal concerns.

Before discussing those legal concerns, it is important to note from the onset that the government, and specifically DHS, has ample legal authority to *receive* voluntarily[266] shared cyberinformation. For example, under Section 201 of the Homeland Security Act, the I&A is authorized to "receive ... information ... [from] private sector entities ... in support of the mission responsibilities of" DHS.[267] Moreover, the NCPA provided explicit statutory authority for the NCCIC to serve as an "interface for the *multi-directional* ... sharing of information related to cybersecurity risks, incidents, analysis, and warnings.... "[268] More broadly, the Critical Infrastructure Information Act (CIIA), a subtitle within the Homeland Security Act, has extensive provisions regarding the treatment of "critical infrastructure information" that is "voluntarily submitted to a ... federal agency",[269] reflecting an assumption that the federal government is not precluded from receiving from a private entity voluntarily shared information pertaining to critical infrastructure.[270]

Freedom of Information Act Disclosures

One central concern for those private entities that may wish to share cyber-intelligence with the government is that the information shared, which may include proprietary information or even simply embarrassing material,[271] could be disclosed through the Freedom of Information Act (FOIA), whether through an affirmative agency disclosure or through a public request.[272] FOIA generally provides that government agencies "shall make available to the public" certain agency records, except insofar as the records are protected from disclosure under several exemptions to the Act.[273] Congress, in the CIIA, provided an exemption to FOIA for any "critical infrastructure information" (CII)[274] that is "voluntarily submitted" to DHS[275] for use by that agency regarding the "security of critical infrastructure" and related purposes.[276] In turn, DHS, through administrative regulations, has created the Protected Critical Infrastructure Information (PCII) Program to ensure that information that is voluntarily shared with the agency receives the protections created by the CIIA.[277]

For those private entities concerned that cyber-intelligence shared with the government will be indiscriminately disseminated through a FOIA request, there are three central concerns with the state of the current law with respect to FOIA and cyber-information sharing. First, the FOIA exemption contained in the CIIA is limited to information that relates to "critical infrastructure,"[278] a term that is confined to only those "systems and assets" that are "vital" to the United States and whose "incapacity or destruction" would have some sort of "debilitating impact" on the country.[279] In other words, unless a private entity is involved with the "backbone of our nation's economy, security and health,"[280] any cyber-information a private entity shares with the federal government would not fall under the FOIA exemption provided in the CIIA.

Second, even if an entity sharing information with DHS is involved with "critical infrastructure," the potential exists that not all cyber-information falls within the CIIA's protections. Instead, only "critical infrastructure information" is exempt from FOIA,[281] a phrase that, while fairly broad in scope, is not limitless.[282] For example, the Homeland Security Act facially limits CII to "information related to the *security* of critical infrastructure,"[283] which could arguably exclude information pertaining to a cyberattack that is not intended to disable or destroy a critical infrastructure system, such as an attack aiming to commit economic espionage.[284] Accordingly, private actors may question whether particular threat information falls within the CIIA's definition for CII, arguably creating legal uncertainty to those who wish to share cyberinformation with the federal government.[285]

Finally, the PCII program created by DHS has a host of various procedural rules that a private entity must follow to ensure that the information provided to DHS receives protections under the CIIA. For example, any CII, to avoid being disclosed under FOIA, will need to be submitted to DHS's PCII Program Manager and will need to contain several certifications and disclaimers,[286] even if the information has been already submitted to another DHS entity, like the NCCIC. As one commentator has noted, the PCII Program's procedural restrictions "necessarily add an extra layer of process that may be sufficient to ultimately defeat the purpose of near real-time information sharing,"[287] if the restrictions do not defeat cyber-information sharing efforts entirely.[288]

It should be noted, however, that just because cyber-intelligence that is provided to DHS may be excluded from the *CIAA's* FOIA exemption that does not necessarily mean that the information will necessarily be disclosed to the public. Indeed, FOIA contains several broad exemptions that may prevent the release of shared cyber-intelligence even if the information does not fall within DHS's definition of PCII.[289] For example, FOIA does not apply to material that involves "trade secrets" or otherwise "privileged or confidential" "commercial or financial information."[290] Nonetheless, without a broader exemption for cyber-information shared with the government, an argument can be made that private cyber-threat information that could contain sensitive material may be disclosed more broadly through FOIA.

Intellectual Property Concerns

Related to the concern about cyber-information sharing and FOIA is the more general concern that cyber-intelligence, once shared with the government, could waive all intellectual property rights associated with such information.[291] The primary body of intellectual property law that could be implicated by cyber-intelligence sharing is trade secret law. The law of trade secrets, which aims to encourage companies and individuals to invest in collecting information that could help secure competitive advantages in the marketplace, protects against the disclosures of "any formula, pattern, device, or compilation of information which is used in one's business and which gives [that business] an opportunity to obtain an advantage over competitors who do not know or use it."[292] Put another way, information is protected as a trade secret to the extent that information (1) has independent value because the information is not generally known and (2) is the subject of efforts to maintain its secrecy.[293] If any person or entity attempts to misappropriate a trade secret, a court can issue injunctive relief or monetary damages against such a defendant.[294]

A private entity, by sharing cyber-intelligence with the government, could risk losing trade secret protection for any valued information that is associated with the cyber-intelligence. For example, when a company shares information about a particular cyber-incident with the government, that entity may be divulging information about internal business operations or disclosing details about the underlying proprietary data that may have been stolen during the course of a cyberattack.[295] The failure to take reasonable steps to prevent gratuitous disclosures of trade secret information forfeits any protection afforded under the law,[296] and the voluntary disclosure of information to a third party generally erodes any trade secret protection for that information.[297]

While the disclosure of cyber-threat information in an unprotected forum—whether public or private—likely risks trade secret protections for that information, in the context of a private entity sharing cyber-intelligence with another party, contractual terms can be negotiated between the parties to provide protections for the intellectual property rights associated with shared cyberintelligence.[298] With respect to sharing cyber-intelligence with the federal government, some have raised concerns about how well the agreements between the government and private entities protect trade secret information that is disclosed in the course of exchanging cyber-intelligence.[299] Specifically, according to DHS, in order to gain access to NCCIC's cyber-intelligence information, a private entity must sign a Cooperative Research and Development Agreement (CRADA) with the agency,[300] and the text of the information-sharing CRADA reportedly includes language that potentially forfeits intellectual property rights in the shared material.[301] Regardless of whether a CRADA could be altered to avoid using such language or whether such language is just the natural result of sharing cyber-information among several public and private actors, as Gregory Garcia, former Assistant Secretary of DHS for Cybersecurity, noted, the CRADAs governing cyber-information sharing "cause[] some companies a lot of heartburn and ... will prevent them from participating or if they do participate they might not do so as robustly if that intellectual property provision did not exist."[302]

Regulatory Enforcement Concerns

Perhaps the primary concern amongst private actors interested in sharing cyber-intelligence with the government is that government regulators will either be "tipped off" because of the shared information and begin an investigation or will "use shared information" as evidence in a regulatory "action against a company."[303] The fear that the government will use information that a private entity shared for cybersecurity purposes *against* that entity may be particularly pronounced if the underlying information pertains to a cyber-breach that resulted in the loss of personal or regulated data.[304]

For example, over the past decade, the FTC, which generally is tasked under the Federal Trade Commission Act with promoting economic competition and consumer protection by eliminating acts or practices that are "unfair or deceptive,"[305] has been at the forefront of federal cybersecurity efforts. In particular, the independent agency has initiated several enforcement actions under Section 5 of the FTC Act that have resulted in tens of millions of dollars in civil penalties, more than fifty private settlements, and expensive compliance obligations for the companies investigated.[306] Some have suggested that the FTC could learn from cyber-intelligence that was shared with DHS that a company has failed to take proper cybersecurity measures, resulting in an FTC investigation of the company.[307] And, perhaps such a scenario is not purely theoretical. In 2010, a cyber-intelligence company shared information with the government that a Georgia-based medical laboratory called LabMD had allowed the billing information for nearly 9,000 patients to be accessed on a peer-to-peer network service, and, in turn, the FTC used the shared information to commence an investigation against LabMD.[308]

In addition to the FTC, the other primary federal agency often mentioned as having an interest in taking regulatory actions as a result of shared cyber-intelligence is the Securities and Exchange Commission (SEC), an independent regulatory agency authorized to administer the Securities Act of 1933 and the Securities Exchange Act of 1934.[309] The two laws are generally aimed at ensuring that investors receive adequate information about the securities being offered to the public for sale and preventing deceit, misrepresentations, and other fraud in the sale of securities.[310] In this vein, the two laws contain detailed disclosure requirements for the sale of securities to the public, including the need for companies to file initial registration statements and periodic reports with the SEC.[311]

Under SEC guidelines, corporations and attorneys are advised to report material cyber-risks and incidents to the SEC.[312] Material cyber-risks and incidents might include new expenditures on corporate cybersecurity, loss of intellectual property, or incidents that have adverse impacts on customers or clients or even that cause "reputational damage adversely affecting customer or investor confidence."[313] Because the failure to disclose material information to the SEC could prompt investigations led by the Commission, risking civil liability and even criminal penalties for the companies involved,[314] a fear exists that information disclosed by a company to the government as part of a cyber-information sharing arrangement, such as details about a cyberbreach, could be used as evidence to show that the company withheld material information from the SEC.[315]

Current law provides fairly limited assurances that shared cyber-intelligence will not be subsequently used by the FTC, SEC, or any other government entity that could use such disclosures in the course of a regulatory enforcement action.[316] Under the CIIA, CII disclosed to DHS cannot be used by "any other Federal, State, or local authority, or any third person, in any civil action arising under Federal or State law" if the information was submitted in "good faith."[317] Moreover, the CIIA prohibits CII from being used or disclosed by "any officer or employee of the United States for purposes other" than (1) for the "purposes [of the CIIA]"; (2) in furtherance of an investigation or the prosecution of a criminal act; or (3) when the information is disclosed to Congress, or its representatives, or the Comptroller General, or its representatives.[318]

The latter provision, if violated by an officer or employee of the United States could result in criminal penalties or loss of employment.[319] Nonetheless, the CIIA's prohibitions on the collateral use of certain cyber-information suffer from many of the shortcomings of the CIIA's FOIA exemption—namely, the limited scope of the term "CII" and the potential obstacles posed by DHS's requirements under the PCII Program.[320] Moreover, phrases like "good faith" and "purposes [of the CIIA]" are not defined by the Act, and there is no case law interpreting the collateral use restrictions of the CIIA, leaving considerable ambiguity as to the scope of those provisions.[321]

Privacy Concerns

Related to the concerns from those in the private sector that the government may use (or misuse) information obtained from cyber-information sharing for a regulatory purpose are broader worries about divulging large volumes of often-sensitive cyber-intelligence to the government. These concerns may be particularly worrisome in the wake the 2013 unauthorized disclosures of classified information by Edward Snowden, a former National Security Agency (NSA) contractor, regarding the size and scope of American foreign intelligence efforts.[322] Many of these disclosures revealed that the government had access to wide swaths of information about the customers of several technology giants, harming those firms' relationships with their customers and reportedly harming the firms' bottom lines.[323] As a result, in the words of one commentator, the "big consequence of Edward Snowden's NSA leaks" may be that companies that would have otherwise been interested in sharing cyber-intelligence with the government "will be extremely wary of anything that has the words 'government' and 'information sharing' so close together."[324] While most of privacy concerns from the private sector regarding sharing cyber-information with the government are non-legal in nature—that is, the debates center on whether information sharing *should* occur given the concerns for personal privacy, not on whether information sharing with the government *can* occur as a result of current federal privacy laws—some have voiced concerns over whether the Stored Communications Act allows for private entities to voluntarily share certain cyber-information with the government.[325]

The SCA was discussed earlier in this report in the context of a service provider disclosing the *contents* of electronic communications to another private entity for cybersecurity purposes.[326] While the content based restrictions contained in Section 2702(a)(1)-(2) apply equally to electronic communications that are shared with the government and, therefore, raise similar legal issues to those discussed above,[327] the SCA also contains a provision explicitly regulating the dissemination of *non-content* information to governmental entities.[328]

Specifically, under 18 U.S.C. Section 2702(a)(3), providers of a RCS or an ECS to the public[329] are generally prohibited from "knowingly divulging a record or other information pertaining to a subscriber or customer of such service ... to any governmental entity."[330] The SCA provides no definition for what "record[s] or other information pertaining to a subscriber or customer" entail,[331] leading to some dispute about the scope of the SCA's prohibition on non-content information. Courts have interpreted "record information" to have a broad import that at the very least includes information like a subscriber's name, identity, address, and communication records, and *may* include broader information that merely relates to a customer or subscriber.[332] The DOJ has issued a White Paper that attempts to cabin the type of "record information" falling within Section 2702(a)(3)'s prohibition to information that "can identify or otherwise provide information about any particular subscriber or customer."[333] In other words, in the view of the Justice Department, private entities can divulge to the government information like the "characteristics of a computer virus or malicious cyber tool" or aggregate information about Internet traffic patterns without running afoul of 18 U.S.C. Section 2702(a)(3).[334] Putting aside the merits of DOJ's position[335]—one commentator has suggested that the SCA's prohibitions on the disclosure of electronic communications to the government "could be and is being construed by many to include the coding of viruses and malware and the IP addresses from which cyber attacks are originating"[336]—the fact that a dispute remains over the scope of the SCA's prohibition on disclosures to the government arguably indicates there is considerable uncertainty as to whether federal privacy law generally prohibits many forms of cyber-intelligence sharing with the government.[337] Like its general prohibitions pertaining to the disclosures made by providers of ECS or RCS to other private entities, the SCA's prohibition respecting disclosures made by service providers to the government has several exceptions,[338] which arguably do little to clarify the legal landscape for those interested in sharing cyber-information with the government. For example, the SCA contains a provider exception and a consent exception for disclosures made by a service provider to the government.[339] As noted above, the SCA's provider exception may only extend to allow for the disclosure of information that is directly related to protecting the rights or property of the *provider*, as opposed to third parties' interests.[340] And the scope of the consent exception will often be tied to the specific facts respecting a particular customer's agreement to allow the service provider to submit cyber-intelligence to the government.[341]

The SCA does contain a third exception specific to disclosures to the government: the Act allows disclosures of content and non-content information to be made by a provider if the provider believes in "good faith" that an "emergency involving danger of death or serious physical injury to any person requires disclosure without delay" of the communications or information "relating to the emergency."[342]

The SCA's "exigent circumstances" exception, however, is an exception that has been read narrowly to allow the government to access information necessary to "prevent or minimize" a true, active emergency and extends no further.[343] It is unclear whether many types of cyber-information in the hands of the private sector would reveal information that would help alleviate an active emergency situation so that the intelligence could be disclosed to the government under the SCA's exigent circumstances exception.

More broadly, given the ambiguities associated with the SCA's general prohibition on voluntary disclosures to the government with regard to electronic communications and the exceptions to that prohibition, much like other areas of law regarding cyber-information sharing, federal privacy law as it pertains to the dissemination of cyber-intelligence from the private sector to the federal government raises many questions and has few clear answers.

LEGISLATIVE OPTIONS FOR CYBER-INFORMATION SHARING

Given the two major categories of cyber-information sharing—sharing of information in the possession of the government and sharing of information in the possession of the private sector— and the myriad of legal issues arising with respect to each category, legislative changes to federal law that aims to encourage the dissemination of cybersecurity information among the public and private sectors could take countless forms. Indeed, during the 113th and 114th Congresses, several legislative proposals have been introduced that aim to remove the current legal obstacles that may be preventing more robust cyber-intelligence sharing, whether by removing discrete legal barriers to information sharing[344] or by effectuating more wholesale change with regard to the distribution of cyber-intelligence within the public and private sectors.[345] While any one of the various legislative proposals on cybersecurity information sharing could merit a lengthy discussion, six themes permeate the various proposals aimed at promoting cybersecurity information sharing— one overarching theme, two that pertain to cyber-information possessed by the government, and three that pertain to cyber-information in the control of the private sector.

Creating a Broader Legal Framework for the Sharing of Cyber-Information

A central difficulty with the current law on cyber-security information is simply that there is very little federal law on the subject. The only federal law that directly contemplates the concept of the federal government and private entities sharing cyber-intelligence with each other is the Homeland Security Act,[346] and that law, by its very terms, is generally limited to the sharing of cybersecurity information as it pertains to critical infrastructure systems.[347] As a result of the lack of any federal framework to guide public and private entities interested in sharing cyberintelligence, the law must be guided by several disparate areas of law whose guiding principles may be antithetical to the widespread dissemination of cyber-intelligence.[348]

To provide clarity to an area of law much in need of clarification, several proposals begin by squarely authorizing some degree of sharing of cyber-intelligence between the public sector and the private sector and between private entities. For example, the Cyber Intelligence Sharing and Protection Act (CISPA), a bill that has passed the House of Representatives the past two Congresses, would explicitly authorize (1) the federal government to "facilitate information sharing, interaction, and collaboration" between the federal government and the private sector,[349] and (2) private sector cybersecurity providers and entities that protect their own information networks to "share cyber threat information with any other entity" of their choosing, including certain entities within the federal government.[350] Similarly, the Cyber Threat Sharing Act of 2015 (CTSA) would allow (1) the NCCIC to "receive and disclose cyber threat indicators" to the rest of the federal government and the private sector,[351] and (2) private entities to share "cyber threat indicators" with certain private sector organizations and the NCCIC.[352]

Having created a general framework that contemplates broader cybersecurity information sharing, the legislative proposals on cybersecurity information sharing *begin* to diverge on three central issues: (1) the *types* of cybersecurity information that is authorized for dissemination within the private sector and between the private and public sectors; (2) the *entities* that can *receive* such information; and (3) the *purposes* for which such information can be used.

- **Types of Cybersecurity Information:** The broadest approach is epitomized by bills like the Cybersecurity Information Sharing Act of 2014 (CISA), which would allow entities to share information about (1) cyber-vulnerabilities, (2) cyber-threats, *and* (3) broader efforts and strategies that have been used to prevent or mitigate cyberattacks,[353] encompassing nearly any type of information within an entity's possession that merely pertains to cybersecurity. A more narrow approach would be that of proposals like the (CTSA), which allows public and private entities to share only limited types of cyber-threat information and does not contemplate entities sharing cybersecurity strategies with each other.[354]
- **Who Can Receive Covered Cybersecurity Information:** Bills like CISPA, which generally authorizes a private entity to share cyber-intelligence with "any other entity" it so chooses,[355] contrast sharply with proposals like the CTSA, which limits sharing by private parties to ISAOs and the NCCIC[356] and does not contemplate sharing of cyber-information between, for example, two private entities outside of an ISAO.
- **Purposes For Which Shared Covered Cyber-Information Can Be Used:** CISPA, for example, allows the disclosing entity to place "any restrictions" on the use of shared information[357] and generally[358] limits shared intelligence so that such material can only be used for a "cybersecurity purpose,"[359] a term of art that broadly encompasses nearly any effort that is aimed at protecting a system or network from

> a range of different cyberattacks.[360] In contrast, the CTSA more closely circumscribes the uses for which shared information can be put. The CTSA, in addition to having provisions analogous to CISPA that limit the use of covered cyber-information based on the restrictions imposed by the sharing entity[361] and general cybersecurity purposes,[362] would affirmatively require those that share and use "cyber threat indicators" to make "reasonable efforts" to minimize information unrelated to a cyber-threat that may be used to identify specific persons and to "safeguard information" that may be used to identify specific persons from unintended or unauthorized disclosures.[363]

The issues of *what* can be shared, with *whom* covered information can be shared, and the *purposes* for which that information can be used once shared will necessarily define the scope and overall goals of any cybersecurity information sharing legislation. Proposals that sharply circumscribe the types of information that can be shared, the parties that can receive such information, and the uses for that information once it is received will necessarily discourage the dissemination and utilization of cyber-intelligence when compared to bills that take a different approach. On the other hand, proposals that generally authorize vast amounts of cyberinformation to be disseminated to a wide range of public and private entities to be used for any number of purposes may be open to criticism that such proposals go too far and undermine other interests, like individual privacy rights. Nonetheless, the three central issues animating the legal frameworks for cybersecurity information reform proposals are only the starting points for the legal discussions on cyber-information reforms. Generally the major proposals on cyberintelligence sharing begin by establishing fairly broad authorizations for the dissemination of cyber-intelligence and then regulate such activities accordingly,[364] creating several other avenues for legal debate.

Clarifying Which Government Agency Leads the Efforts on CyberInformation Sharing

Once a legislative proposal has generally authorized broader cybersecurity information sharing between the public and private sectors, the legislation may need to resolve what entity in the government needs to be the liaison between the public and private sector with regard to such sharing of information. As noted above, while ample legal authority currently exists for DHS to serve as the central repository and distributor of cyber-intelligence for the federal government,[365] the legal authorities that do exist often overlap, perhaps resulting in confusion as to which of the multiple sub-agencies within DHS or even outside of DHS, like the newly formed CTICC, should be leading efforts on cybersecurity information sharing.[366]

While earlier versions of cybersecurity legislation contemplated placing the Office of the Director of National Intelligence (DNI) or the Department of Defense (DOD) at the forefront of federal cyber-information sharing efforts,[367] more recent legislation has tasked DHS with the role of coordinating cyber-information sharing. For example, the CTSA designates the NCCIC as the entity charged with receiving and disclosing all "cyber threat indicators" to federal and nonfederal entities.[368] Less specific, CISPA allows the President to designate an "entity within [DHS] as the civilian Federal entity to receive cyber threat information"[369] and share that information with other governmental entities,[370] while allowing the President to designate an entity within DOJ to serve as the entity that receives information related to cybercrimes[371] and disseminates such information throughout the federal government.[372] Other legislation may attempt to task *several* federal agencies with the job of promulgating regulations with respect to the receipt and distribution of cyber-intelligence. CISA, for example, would require the DNI, DHS, DOD, and DOJ to consult and jointly develop procedures that facilitate the timely sharing of federal "cyber threat indicators."[373] The bill would also require the Attorney General to promulgate "policies and procedures" with regard to the receipt of cyber-threat indicators form the private sector.[374] Nonetheless, CISA does contemplate a central role for DHS with regard to the receipt and disclosure of cyber-information, requiring the agency to "develop and implement a capability and process" for accepting cyber threat indicators and countermeasures and ensuring all appropriate federal entities "receive such cyber threat indicators.... "[375]

Few proposals, however, would attempt to resolve the issue of overlapping legal authorities that currently exist with respect to cyber-information sharing. While an argument could be made that the CTSA's naming of the NCCIC as the entity charged with receiving and distributing cyber threat indicators clarifies internal divisions of authority as to what agencies must take the lead on cyber-information sharing efforts,[376] nothing in the legislation explicitly repeals similar authority provided to other federal entities in earlier laws, implying that such authorities remain.[377] Other proposals, such as CISPA, go so far as to disclaim "limit[ing] or modify[ing]" "existing" information sharing relationships,[378] indicating that such proposals would do little to modify the existing division of authority within the federal government with respect to cybersecurity information sharing.

Increasing the Amount and Quality of Government Cyber-Information Disclosed to the Private Sector

Beyond clarifying *who* in the government is tasked with receiving and disseminating cyberinformation, another central theme for cybersecurity proposals is ensuring that the underlying information that is disseminated from the government is both voluminous and helpful. As discussed above, while the government has wide authority to disclose cyber-intelligence within its possession, that authority is not limitless and is necessarily tied to laws that restrict the government's ability to release sensitive information within its possession.[379] More broadly, delays in the dissemination and sanitation of cyber-intelligence arguably may severely diminish the effectiveness of such information.[380]

To increase the speed at which cyber-threat information is distributed and the volume of cyberintelligence that is disclosed, two main strategies are contemplated by various cybersecurity proposals. First, several pieces of cybersecurity legislation would require DHS to create the capabilities to distribute cyber-intelligence in "real time" to other federal agencies[381] and even the private sector.[382] CISA, for example, contemplates real time or instantaneous, "automated" distribution of cyber-information being facilitated through the creation of a universal electronic format for cyber-information.[383] Second, several bills contemplate authorizing additional access to classified cyber-intelligence within the possession of the government by those in the private sector.[384] For example, CISPA mandates that the DNI establish procedures to allow the intelligence community to share classified cyber-threat intelligence with the private sector,[385] including requiring the expedited issuance of security clearances for those who may need access to cyber-intelligence.[386]

Nonetheless, most of the proposals encouraging faster and more robust dissemination of cyberinformation speak only in the most general terms and delegate the authority to accomplish, for example, real time dissemination of cyber-information to an agency like DHS or the DNI.[387] There is an inherent tension between (1) allowing for the rapid disclosure of a large volume of sensitive cyber-intelligence and (2) preserving the privacy and national security interests that currently limit the disclosure of such information. What remains to be seen is whether legislation or subsequent agency action can effectively accomplish the competing goals that underlie the debate over recent cybersecurity information sharing efforts.

Minimizing Liability Related to Distributing Privately Held CyberIntelligence

Perhaps the most heavily debated legal issue respecting cyber-information sharing legislation is how to adequately minimize the host of liability issues that may arise for those in the private sector that may wish to disclose cyber-intelligence to outsiders.[388] As noted above, those in the private sector that wish to engage in cyber-information sharing may be exposed to civil and even criminal liability from a host of different federal and state laws.[389] Moreover, because of the uncertainty that pervades the interplay between laws of general applicability—like federal antitrust or privacy law—and their specific application to cyber-intelligence sharing, it may be very difficult for any private entity to accurately assess potential liability that could arise by participating in a sharing scheme.[390] Without some assurances with regard to liability, the potential exists that a private entity may simply refuse to participate in information sharing, reasoning that any amorphous benefits that could be realized would simply not cover the cost of liability.[391] As a consequence, several cybersecurity proposals have attempted to minimize potential exposure for and rationalize any costs associated with sharing privately held cyberintelligence,[392] initiating a legal debate of its very own on how to properly scope such liability protections.[393]

"Tailored" Approach to Minimizing Liability

There are two central legal approaches to crafting liability immunity provisions in the context of cybersecurity information sharing legislation. First, some have argued for including more narrowly tailored immunity provisions, such that a provision is tied to a particular law that could be the source of civil or criminal liability for private entities that engage in cyber-information sharing.[394] For example, Gregory Nojeim of the Center for Democracy and Technology has argued for passing legislation that creates an additional exemption to ECPA, authorizing service providers to "make disclosures to other service providers or to the government to help protect the systems of *other* service providers."[395]Likewise, others have advocated for a "cyber-security exception to the antitrust laws," by creating an explicit "legislative carve-out" allowing for the exchange of "vulnerability, threat, and countermeasure information and the development of common security protocols."[396] The upside of the "tailored" approach to liability protection is that by crafting narrow immunity provisions there is less of a risk that any new cybersecurity legislation will disrupt or undermine the goals of previously existing legislative schemes by, for example, immunizing anticompetitive behavior or actions that erode third-party privacy interests.

Nonetheless, the tailored immunity approach has a significant drawback, as well, in that crafting an immunity provision for each and every source of liability that a private entity could face with regard to the sharing of cyber-intelligence may simply be impossible. After all, those entities that collect or disclose cybersecurity information could potentially face countless lawsuits arising under (1) any of the three titles of ECPA, (2) any of a number of other federal privacy laws, (3) federal antitrust law, (4) state common law tort, fiduciary duty, or implied contract claims, or (5) a variety of state privacy or antitrust laws.[397] An argument can be made many of these legal claims are simply meritless or inapplicable with respect to the most benign forms of a cyberintelligence sharing. Nonetheless, the fact remains that at least in the view of many information technology experts significant gray areas exist in various places in the law deterring more aggressive forms of cyber-intelligence sharing,[398] perhaps warranting more broad-based liability protections. Moreover, because of the potential bases for civil liability, like antitrust and tort law, are based in part on evolving common law standards, enacting cybersecurity information sharing legislation that includes a narrowly tailored immunity provision may not deter the lawsuits of tomorrow that are unanticipated by lawmakers.[399] Finally, even if many of the legal claims levied against entities that share cyber-threat information may be meritless, a determination of the legal merits will often require factual development by the litigants, as federal litigants, for example, need only plead a plausible theory as to liability in order to avoid the initial dismissal of a federal complaint.[400] As a result, liability carve-outs that are limited to only the most meritorious legal claims may not prevent private entities from being subject to potentially expensive factual discovery that may deter cybersecurity information sharing efforts.[401]

"Broad" Approach to Minimizing Liability

Perhaps as a result of the drawbacks of the tailored approach, most of the recent legislation on cybersecurity information sharing has taken the opposite approach: proposing more sweeping language that broadly immunizes private entities involved in collecting and disclosing cyberintelligence and then drafting tailored exceptions to curb the scope of the immunity. The "broad" approach to civil liability protections for those that wish to collect and share cybersecurity information commonly has four foundations:

- **Notwithstanding Clauses:** Several cybersecurity bills, in authorizing the collection or sharing of cyber-information, will preface any such language with a "notwithstanding" clause.[402] For example, Section 3 of CISA states "Notwithstanding any other provision of law, an entity may ... share with, or receive from, any other entity or the Federal Government cyber threat indicators and countermeasures."[403] Courts generally interpret notwithstanding clauses as signifying that any phrases following the clause "supplant" and "supersede" any conflicting law,[404] which in the context of cybersecurity legislation would imply that any authorizing language to collect and disseminate covered cyber-information that followed a notwithstanding clause would supersede any laws of general applicability that may deter or prohibit such behavior.
- **Limitation of Liability Clauses:** Beyond the use of notwithstanding clauses, recent cybersecurity legislation has additionally contained explicit provisions that pertain to liability and contemplate dismissal of lawsuits at early stages of litigation generally pertaining to cyber-information collection and/or sharing.[405]
- **Good Faith Safe Harbors:** In addition to explicit liability limitations, CISPA and CISA both contain provisions that would allow defendants whose conduct otherwise would not fall within the scope of the limitation of liability clause to seek dismissal on the ground that the defendant relied in good faith that the conduct complained of was "permitted" under the law.[406]
- **Preemption Clauses:** Finally, to ensure that no *state* or *local* laws interfere with cybersecurity information sharing, recent cybersecurity proposals have contained explicit preemption clauses that functionally displace any non-federal laws that could be the source of liability for or otherwise interfere with any activities permitted under a given cyber-information sharing proposal.[407]

The broad approach to liability protections for private entities that collect and disseminate cyberintelligence should not be conflated with a "limitless" approach. Rather the scope of the immunity provisions under the broad approach is necessarily a product of language contained within the four key clauses. As a consequence, cybersecurity bills vary considerably with respect to the scope of liability protections for information sharing. For example, CTSA only prohibits civil or criminal causes of action from being maintained against entities for receiving or disclosing "lawfully obtained cyber threat indicators" from the NCCIC or a self-certified ISAO.[408] The plain language of the CTSA would not immunize an entity with regard to (1) activities taken to *acquire* cyber-threat information; (2) the sharing of information outside of the NCCIC or a self-certified ISAO; or (3) if the underlying information were not "lawfully obtained cyber threat indicators," which presumably would exclude from the provision "cyber threat indicators" for which "reasonable efforts" had not been made to eliminate personal information from such information.[409] In contrast, bills like CISA more broadly prohibit causes of action based on the collection, sharing, or receipt of information with any other entity or the federal government.[410] Moreover, beyond the general language respecting the four key clauses pertaining to immunity, legislative proposals may have specific carve-outs that pertain to a given cause of action, such as provisions in CISA that maintain antitrust claims based on "price-fixing" or "monopolization"[411] or tort claims based on "gross negligence" or "willful misconduct."[412] The question that remains to be answered with respect to the broad approach toward liability protection is whether such an approach will truly accomplish the goals of minimizing exposure and creating more legal certainty for those private parties that may wish to share cyberintelligence. Given the host of limits and caveats that have been placed on the general immunity provisions in the various cybersecurity bills, one might ask whether the resulting language creates a host of new legal questions and produces an equally uncertain legal landscape as to the liability risks posed by information sharing. More broadly, phrases like "good faith" and "notwithstanding" are arguably not legal silver bullets that will necessarily eliminate all litigation associated with cyber-information collection and sharing.[413] Nonetheless, given that legal certainty may simply be impossible with respect to an activity at the epicenter of so many areas of law, the ultimate questions for lawmakers with respect to information sharing immunity provisions will be how much legal uncertainty can be tolerated by the private sector and how much of a role should other laws—like federal privacy and antitrust laws—play with regard to cyber-intelligence collection and dissemination.

Increasing the Participation of Private Sector Cyber-Information Sharing

Questions respecting liability protections in cybersecurity legislation take place in a broader debate over how to increase the participation of private sector entities that currently may be reluctant to share cyber-intelligence within their possession. One solution that has been suggested is to amend current law on cybersecurity information sharing, which contemplates private entities *voluntarily* sharing and receiving information,[414] and impose a mandate on entities to collect cyber-intelligence from their own computer networks and share it with other private entities and the government or else risk civil liability for refusal to comply with the mandate.[415]

Mandatory information sharing could raise several difficult legal questions, however. First, a mandate that companies collect and share cyber-information could be in tension with the Fourth Amendment to the Constitution, which generally prohibits the government from conducting unreasonable searches.[416] While the Fourth Amendment facially only applies to government searches,[417] courts have recognized that searches conducted by ostensibly private parties can constitute government action when the government knew of and acquiesced in the intrusive conduct and the party performing the search intended the search to occur for the benefit of the government.[418] Arguably, a government mandate to collect cyber-intelligence would transform those in the private sector who are now *required* under federal law to share information with the government into government actors, raising the question of whether such a law would violate the Fourth Amendment.[419] The resolution of that question will likely depend on a number of factors. For example, the Fourth Amendment inquiry will likely depend on the nature of cyber-information being collected in the private sector, as acquisitions of non-content information have generally been found to fall outside of Fourth Amendment protection.[420] Moreover, any Fourth Amendment challenge may fail if the plaintiff consented to the underlying search[421] by, for example, agreeing to a computer-use policy or clicking through a banner on a website that warns of the potential invasion of privacy.[422] Finally, the propriety of a mandatory cyber-information program under the Fourth Amendment may depend on the specifics of a mandatory information sharing program, as the Supreme Court has recognized a "special needs" exception to the Fourth Amendment, whereby when a "special need" beyond the "normal need for law enforcement, make[s] the warrant and probable-cause requirement impracticable"[423]—such as preventing a cyberattack—require balancing the gravity of the public interests, the degree to which an intrusion advances the public interests, and the severity of the interference with individual liberty.[424]

Mandated disclosures of cyber-intelligence may conflict with other provisions in the Constitution. For example, the Supreme Court has recognized that the First Amendment not only protects the "right to speak freely," but also includes "the right to refrain from speaking at all."[425] While much of the Court's compelled speech jurisprudence arises in the context of a speaker being forced to endorse a particular ideological message,[426] the Court has recognized that "compelled statements of fact ... like compelled statements of opinion, are subject to First Amendment scrutiny."[427] In the context of requiring a private entity to disclose cyber-information, an argument could be made that a private entity has a First Amendment interest in not being required to divulge factual information the entity "would rather avoid."[428] While the Court has upheld compelled disclosure requirements in context of commercial speech cases,[429] it is unclear whether commercial speech case law is relevant to the compelled disclosure of cyber-intelligence.[430] Instead, content-based speech compelled by the government is generally subject to strict scrutiny, requiring the underlying policy to be narrowly tailored to promote a compelling government interest.[431] Given the serious threat potentially posed by cyberattacks and the supposed ability of robust cyberintelligence to deter such attacks,[432] a narrowly tailored mandate for the disclosure of cyberthreats arguably may be able to survive a First Amendment challenge.[433] Nonetheless, the law on compelled speech is far from clear[434] and may be one of several other constitutional challenges to a mandatory cyber-threat collection and disclosure law.[435]

Beyond the constitutional issues respecting mandatory cyber-information sharing, there may be practical problems with such a proposal. For example, imposing some sort of penalty or liability on a company that did not participate in a mandatory information sharing scheme only induces an entity to share information if the penalties for not participating outweigh costs associated with participation, such as liability risks or risks to a firm's reputation for disclosing the details about a cyberattack.[436] Moreover, as one commentator has argued, because of the prevalence of consumer and privacy groups closely watching those that possess cybersecurity information, voluntary cyber-information sharing programs can be better tailored than heavy-handed mandates to ensure that information is shared in a manner that is effective, but not so robust as to allow for "forms of sharing that the public believes are especially intrusive."[437]

Recent cybersecurity legislation has eschewed any mandatory information sharing schemes. For example, CISPA contains an "anti-tasking restriction" that explicitly prevents the bill from being construed to "require a private-sector entity or utility to share information with the Federal Government."[438] Similar provisions exist in the CTSA[439] and CISA.[440] The issue that remains for lawmakers who prefer a voluntary scheme for cyber-information sharing is how to create sufficient incentives that overcome the legal and non-legal disincentives that are currently deterring more robust dissemination of cyber-intelligence.[441] Proposals like CISPA provide two related incentives—liability protections and access to government cyber-intelligence—but other incentives for information sharing could include subsidies,[442] such as "direct payments from the government, tax credits, or deductions" for entities that engage in cyber-information sharing,[443] or other benefits like intellectual property protections.[444] At least one bill has been introduced in Congress that would amend the Internal Revenue Code to create incentives for information sharing.[445] Whether any or all of these incentives would be effective in increasing participation in cyber-intelligence sharing schemes, an issue beyond the scope of this report, will be a critical question for lawmakers to resolve when considering any cybersecurity legislation that aims to increase the amount of cyber-threat information that is available within the private sector.[446]

Preventing Government Misuse of Acquired Cyber-Intelligence

Finally, the last major issue for cybersecurity information sharing legislation is to assuage public fears associated with the government collecting privately held cyber-intelligence, including concerns that the information disclosed to the government could (1) be released through a FOIA request; (2) result in the forfeiting of certain intellectual property rights; (3) be used against a private entity in a subsequent regulatory action; or (4) risk the privacy rights of individuals whose information may be encompassed in disclosed cyber-intelligence.[447] While each of the major legislative proposals on cyber-information sharing may differ in substance, there is considerable consensus on the *approach* congressional bills have taken with respect to each of the four major concerns over government control of voluntarily disclosed cyber-intelligence:

- **Public Records Disclosures:** Recent cybersecurity legislation has opted to create a broad FOIA exemption, exempting any covered cyber-information that is shared with the federal government from public disclosure.[448] CISPA, for example, states that "[c]yber threat information shared" in line with the requirements of the bill, if shared with the federal government, "shall be exempt from disclosure" under FOIA,[449] whereas CISA exempts from disclosure "[c]yber threat indicators and countermeasures provided to the" federal government under the bill.[450] In other words, the scope of the FOIA exemptions provided under recent proposals necessarily are a product of what sort of information a particular cyber-information sharing bill covers as an initial matter.[451]
- **Intellectual Property Rights Protection:** To prevent intellectual property rights—such as trade secrets rights—in any shared cyber-intelligence from being forfeited upon disclosure to the government, several proposals contain specific provisions disclaiming any loss of rights as a result of information sharing.[452] CISPA declares that cyber-threat information shared in accordance with the bill must "be considered proprietary information" and restricts disclosure of such material to outsiders unless allowed by the disclosing entity,[453] potentially providing those that share cyber-intelligence with the ability to preserve any trade secret rights in such information. CISA may have the most explicit provisions respecting preservation of intellectual property rights for shared cyberintelligence, stating that the "provision of cyber threat indicators and countermeasures" to the government "shall not constitute a waiver of any applicable privilege or protection provided by law, including trade secret protection."[454]
- **Regulatory Enforcement Concerns:** To temper fears that cyber-information that is disclosed to the government will be used in later regulatory enforcement actions, two main strategies have been employed in recent cybersecurity legislation. First, several bills have blanket statements that declare that any covered information that is shared with the government will not be used for "regulatory purposes" or a "regulatory enforcement action,"[455] terms of art that are left undefined by the bills. Second, the various legislative proposals will affirmatively limit the federal government from utilizing the shared information for any purpose other than (1) a "cybersecurity purpose;" (2) to prevent or mitigate an imminent threat of death or serious

bodily harm; (3) to respond, prevent or mitigate a serious threat to a minor; or (4) prevent, investigate, or prosecute certain cybercrimes.[456]

- **Privacy Concerns:** In order to assuage more general privacy-based concerns about the implications of the government collecting cyber-information, recent cybersecurity legislation has generally avoided crafting precise rules respecting privacy within the legislation itself in favor of requiring DHS, in conjunction with other federal agencies, to promulgate procedures, policies, and regulations on the federal handling of disclosed information.[457] The guidance the various legislative proposals provide to DHS for the promulgation of privacy rules is general in nature and is centered on the concern that disclosed cyber-intelligence may contain PII.[458] Nonetheless, some proposals do contain specific rules aimed at restricting what types of cyber-information the government can collect and use. CISPA, for example, prevents the government from "us[ing]" particular sensitive documents that contain PII, such as library circulation records or firearm sales records,[459] and prohibits the government from "affirmatively searching" any collected cyber-threat information.[460] CISA affirmatively requires the federal government to protect shared "cyber threat indicators" from unauthorized use or disclosure that may contain PII.[461]

Given the various restrictions imposed or contemplated in recent cybersecurity information sharing proposals, the issue that remains is how to ensure that such restrictions are complied with by the government. The central enforcement mechanism for any affirmative restrictions on the government's use of shared cyber-information is congressional oversight, in that many of the cyber-information sharing bills require federal agencies to submit regular reports to Congress respecting the government's use of shared cyber-intelligence,[462] including compliance with privacy regulations.[463] Nonetheless, there could be other legal mechanisms available to ensure government compliance with a law's restrictions on the use of shared cyber-intelligence. For example, the CTSA contemplates that any privacy rules promulgated under the proposal would provide for "appropriate penalties for" any government officer, employee, or agent that violates a rule regarding the "receipt, retention, or disclosure of a cyber threat indicator."[464] CISPA perhaps has the most aggressive enforcement mechanism with respect to those government entities that violate the proposal's use restrictions, in that the bill includes a provision that would impose liability on the United States for an intentional or willful violation of any of CISPA's restrictions on how the government can utilize any voluntarily shared cyber-intelligence.[465] Nonetheless, no legislative proposals go as far as current law does with respect to CII, *criminalizing* misconduct with respect to information shared regarding critical infrastructure.[466] Regardless of the enforceability of a particular restriction on the use of cyber-intelligence by the government, a fundamental question lawmakers may need to contemplate is how restrictions that require close government scrutiny and control over shared cyber-information can be squared with other goals of cyber-information sharing legislation, like requirements that received information be disseminated in an almost instantaneous fashion.[467] Ultimately, because the goals of cyberinformation legislation are often diametrically opposed, it may simply be impossible for information sharing legislation to simultaneously promote the rapid and robust collection and dissemination of cyber-intelligence by the federal government, while also ensuring that the government respects the property and privacy interests implicated by such information sharing.[468]

CONCLUSION

The current legal framework surrounding cyber-information sharing exists at the crossroads of several bodies of law and raises complicated questions respecting how cyber-intelligence can be collected and shared within the private sector and with the public sector. Moreover, as demonstrated by the host of discrepancies and complications raised by various legislative proposals on information sharing, if Congress chooses to alter the current legal framework governing cybersecurity and intelligence sharing, the law will not necessarily be devoid of uncertainty. Instead, new legal questions may arise, likely out of the context of the balance Congress attempts to strike between lowering disincentives for information sharing and ensuring that other interests embodied in privacy, antitrust, tort, or other laws are sufficiently protected under new cybersecurity information sharing legislation. While cybersecurity information sharing is, at most, only one piece of a much larger puzzle regarding how to best protect the United States against potentially debilitating cyberattacks,[469] resolution of the difficult legal questions posed by the regulation of cyber-intelligence sharing may be an important task for the 114th Congress.

End Notes

[1] For purposes of this report, the term "cyberattack" refers to a deliberate infiltration of a computer system or network with the intent to either extract or destroy confidential information or to destroy the functioning of the system or network. *See* Jay P. Kesan and Carol M. Hayes, *Mitigative Counterstriking: Self-Defense and Deterrence in Cyberspace*, 25 HARV. J.L. & TECH. 429, 439-446 (2012). It should be noted however the exact contours of what the term "cyberattack" entails is subject to much debate. *See id.* at 439 ("The modern lexicon considers all types of online intrusions to be cyberattacks, even though many commentators would assert that such indiscriminate use of the term 'cyberattack' is incorrect."); *see also* William A. Owens, Kenneth W. Dam, and Herbert S. Lin, et al., *Overview, Findings, and Recommendations*, in TECHNOLOGY, POLICY, LAW, AND ETHICS REGARDING U.S. ACQUISITION AND USE OF CYBERATTACK CAPABILITIES 10-11(2009) (distinguishing between the terms "cyberattack" and "cyber exploitation"); Oona A. Hathaway et al., *The Law of Cyber-Attack*, 100 CALIF. L. REV. 817, 823 (2012). ("The absence of a shared definition has made it difficult for analysts from different countries to develop coordinated policy recommendations and for governments to engage in coordinated actions.")

[2] Malware is the diminutive for malicious software and can come in a wide variety of forms. *See generally* Rick Lehtinen, Deborah Russell, and G.T. Gangemi Sr., COMPUTER SECURITY BASICS 80 (2d ed. 2006); *see also* Matthew J. Skelrov, *Solving the Dilemma of State Responses to Cyberattacks: A Justification for the Use of Active Defenses Against States Who Neglect Their Duty to Prevent*, 201 ML. L. REV. 1, 15 n.78. (2009).

[3] *See* Dan Goodin, Epic Target hack reportedly began with malware-based phishing email, ARS TECHNICA, (February 12, 2014), http://arstechnica.com/security/2014/02/epic-target-hack-reportedly-began-with-malware-based-phishing-email/.

[4] *See* Press Release, *Target Provides Update on Data Breach and Financial Performance,* (January 10, 2014), *available at* http://pressroom.target.com/news/target-provides-update-on-data-breach-and-financial-performance.

[5] *See* Press Release, *eBay Inc. To Ask eBay Users To Change Passwords*, (May 21, 2014), *available at* http://www.ebayinc.com/in_the_news/story/ebay-inc-ask-ebay-users-change-passwords.

[6] *See* Press Release, *The Home Depot Completes Malware Elimination and Enhanced Encryption of Payment Data in All U.S. Stores*, (September 18, 2014), *available at* http://www.prnewswire.com/news-releases/the-home-depotcompletes-malware-elimination-and-enhanced-encryption-of-payment-data-in-all-us-stores-275649511.html.

[7] *See* Emily Glazer and Daniel Yadron, J.*P. Morgan Says About 76 Million Households Affected By Cyber Breach*, WALL STREET JOURNAL (October 2, 2014), *available at* http://www.wsj.com/articles/j-p-morgan-says-about-76-millionhouseholds-affected-by-cyber-breach-1412283372.

[8] See Press Release, Message for current and former Sony Pictures employees and dependents, and for production employees, (December 15, 2014), available at http://www.sonypictures.net/SPE_Cyber_Notification.pdf?.

[9] *See* Amelia Smith, *Sony Cyber Attack One of Worst in Corporate History*, NEWSWEEK, (December 4, 2014), *available at* http://www.newsweek.com/sony-cyber-attack-worst-corporate-history-thousands-files-are-leaked-289230.

[10] *See* Press Release, *Statement regarding cyberattack against Anthem,* (February 11, 2015), *available at* https://www.anthem.com/health-insurance/about-us/pressreleasedetails/WI /2015/1813/statement-regarding-cyberattack-against-anthem.

[11] *See generally Managing cyber risks in an interconnected world,* PRICEWATERHOUSE COOPERS, 5, (September 30, 2014) *available at* http://www.pwc.com/gx/en/consulting-services/information-security-survey/index.jhtml (noting that in a survey of 9,700 security, IT, and business executives in 154 countries, cybersecurity incidents have risen 66% since 2009).

[12] *See 2014: A Year of Mega Breaches,* PONEMON INSTITUTE, 1, (January 2015) *available at* http://www.ponemon.org/ local/upload/file/2014%20The%20Year%20of%20the%20Mega%20Breach%20FINAL3.p df (hereinafter "Ponemon Institute- 2014") (noting breaches at CHS community Health Systems, Michaels Stores, Nieman Marcus, and Staples).

[13] *See* PRICEWATERHOUSE COOPERS, *supra* note 11, at 7 (estimating that globally 117,339 attacks occur each day).

[14] *See Is Your Company Ready for a Big Data Breach?,* PONEMON INSTITUTE, 1, (September 2014), *available at* http://www.experian.com/assets/data-breach/brochures /2014-ponemon-2nd-annual-preparedness.pdf (hereinafter "Ponemon Institute- Big Data Breach"). This study, of course, only accounts for cyberattacks are actually discovered by a given business. One cybersecurity expert estimates that 85% of cyberattacks go unnoticed for two or more weeks. *See* Joshua R. McCloud, *Cisco's Internal Approach to Cyber Security,* (February 2013), *available at* http://www.cisco.com/web/AP/asiapac/academy /Archive/News_ Feb.shtml.

[15] Chenda Ngak, *Are Facebook, Twitter, Apple, New York Times, NBC hacks a sign of things to come?,* CBS NEWS, February 22, 2013, http://www.cbsnews.com/8301-205_162-57570805/are-facebook-twitter-apple-new-york-timesnbc-hacks-a-sign-of-things-to-come/.

[16] *See* Sharone Tobias, *2014: The Year in Cyberattacks,* NEWSWEEK (December 31, 2014), *available at* http://www.newsweek.com/2014-year-cyber-attacks-295876.

[17] *See* Lee Raine, Janna Anderson, and Jennifer Connolly, *Cyber Attacks Likely to Increase,* PEW RESEARCH CENTER, 6- 7 (October 29, 2014), *available at* http://www.pewinternet.org /files/2014/10/ PI_FutureofCyberattacks_102914_pdf.pdf/ (reporting that from a canvass of "thousands of experts and Internet builders," 61% predicted that by 2025 "a major cyber attack [will] cause[] widespread harm to a nation's security and capacity to defend itself and its people"); *see also Threats Report,* MCAFEE LABS, 6-14, (November 2014), *available at* http://www.mcafee.com/us/resources/reports/rp-quarterly-threat-q3-2014.pdf (concluding that cyber threats will increase in the year 2015); *see also* Arjun Khrarpal, *Think 2014 was bad for hacking? Worse is to come,* CNBC (January 15, 2015), *available at* http://www.cnbc.com/id/102362835# (quoting Cisco CEO John Chambers).

[18] *See* PRICEWATERHOUSE COOPERS, *supra* note 11, at 10 (noting that the "annual estimated reported average financial loss attributed to cybersecurity incidents was $2.7 million, a jump of 34% over 2013").

[19] *See* Owens, *supra* note 1, at 9.

[20] See Securing America's Future: The Cyber Security Act of 2012: Hearing on S. 2105 Before the S. Comm. on Homeland Sec. and Gov't Affairs, 112th Cong. (2012) (statement of Michael Chertoff, former Sec'y of the Dep't of Homeland Sec.), available at http://www.hsgac.senate.gov/download/cybersecurity-support-statement-former-dhs-secretary-michael-chertoff.

[21] *See* Joel Brenner, *How Obama Fell Short on Cyber Security,* POLITICO MAGAZINE (January 21, 2015), *available at* http://www.politico.com/magazine/story/2015/01/state-of-the-union-cybersecurity-obama114411.html#.VMlUeXtq3VY (noting the sources for various cyberattacks).

[22] *See* Michael Hayden, Curt Hebert, and Susan Tierney, *Cybersecurity and the North American Electric Grid: New Policy Approaches to Address an Evolving Threat,* BIPARTISAN POLICY CENTER, (February 28, 2014), *available at* http://bipartisanpolicy.org /library/cybersecurity-electric-grid/ ("Cyber threats to North America's electric grid are growing, making electric grid cybersecurity an increasingly important national and international issue.").

[23] *See* Pierluigi Paganini, *Cyber Threats against the Aviation Industry,* INFOSEC INSTITUTE, (April 8, 2014), *available at* http://resources.infosecinstitute.com/cyber-threats-aviation-industry/. ("Security is fundamental for the aviation industry. Considering the availability of numerous tools on the market that could be exploited in a hypothetical attack against a plane, cyber security is becoming even more crucial.")

[24] *See* Jason Koebler, *U.S Nukes Face Up to 10 Million Cyber Attacks Daily,* U.S. NEWS & WORLD REPORT, (March 20, 2014) ("The computer systems of the agency in charge of America's nuclear weapons stockpile are "under constant attack" and face millions of hacking attempts daily").

[25] *See* Leon E. Panetta, Sec'y, U.S. Dep't of Def., *Remarks on Cybersecurity to the Business Executives for National Security,* (October 11, 2012), *available at* http://www.defense.gov/transcripts/transcript.aspx?transcriptid=5136.

[26] *See* Joel Brenner, AMERICA THE VULNERABLE 24 (2011). While there appears to be general agreement about United States' vulnerabilities to a cyberattack, *see* Nathan Sales, *Regulating Cyber-Security,* 107 NW. U. L. REV. 1503, 1505 (2013) ("There are some naysayers but the consensus that we stand on the brink of cyber-calamity is both broad deep."), this viewpoint is not unanimous. *See, e.g.,* Jerry Brito and Tate Watkins, *Loving the Cyber Bomb? The Dangers of Threat Inflation in Cybersecurity Policy*, 3 HARV. NAT. SEC. J. 39 (2011); Vida M. Antolin-Jenkins, Defining the Parameters of Cyberwar Operations: Looking for Law in All the Wrong Places?, 51 NAVAL L. REV. 132, 144-45 (2005).

[27] *See, e.g.,* Steven Dennis, *Obama Pushes for Deals on Cybersecurity, Trade, Taxes,* ROLL CALL (January 13, 2015), *available at* http://blogs.rollcall.com/white-house/obama-meeting-with-top-congressional-leaders-without-harry-reid/? pos=adpb ("Obama says he's spoken to Speaker John A. Boehner, R-Ohio, and Senate Majority Leader Mitch McConnell, R-Ky., on cybersecurity and 'I think we agreed that this is an area where we can work hard together, get some legislation done and make sure that we are much more effective in protecting the American people from these kinds of cyberattacks'").

[28] *See generally* Henry Farrell, *The political science of cybersecurity I—why people fight so hard over cybersecurity*, WASHINGTON POST (January 13, 2014), *available at* http://www.washingtonpost.com/blogs/monkey-cage/wp/2014/01/ 23/the-political-science-of-cybersecurity-i-why-people-fight-so-hard-over-cybersecurity/.

[29] Throughout this report, use of terms "cyber-intelligence," "cyber-information," "cyber-threat information," and "cybersecurity information" are used to holistically capture the entire range of possible information that could help deter or mitigate a cyber-attack, including vulnerability, threat, and countermeasure data. *See infra* note 31 and accompanying text.

[30] *See* Bipartisan Policy Center, *Cyber Security Task Force: Public-Private Information Sharing,* July 2012, at p. 5, *available at* http://bipartisanpolicy.org/wp-content/uploads/sites/default

/files/PublicPrivate%20Information%20Sharing.pdf. This is not to say that there is agreement as to the particulars of how information sharing should be facilitated, such as the need for privacy and civil liberty protections for information shared amongst private and public entities. *See, e.g.*, Erin Kelly, *Obama, Congress may find cybersecurity consensus*, USA TODAY (January 25, 2015), *available at* http://www.usatoday.com/story/news /politics/2015/01/25/cybersecurityinformation-sharing-bill/22229049/ ("That doesn't mean that there are no conflicts between the White House and Congress on the issue. House Republican leaders are still angry that the president threatened to veto an information-sharing bill they passed in the last Congress. Obama said the bill did not do enough to protect the privacy of Americans' personal data in the information-sharing process.").

[31] *See* Sales, *supra* note 26, at 1546. Threat data may consist of "signatures," patterns of network traffic deployed to detect and mitigate malicious cyber-activity, which in turn are comprised of cyber threat "indicators"—a combination of data such as IP addresses, domain names, email headers, files, and internal strings that identify the malicious activity. *See* Jeremy J. Broggi, *Building on Executive Order 13,636 to Encourage Information Sharing for Cybersecurity Purposes*, 37 HARV. J.L. & PUB. POL'Y 653, 657 (2014); *see generally* Lehtinen, *supra* note 1, at 80.

[32] *See* Sales, *supra* note 26, at 1546*; see also* Bipartisan Policy Center, *supra* note 30, at 7 ("With more robust information sharing, there can be greater situational awareness about the health of the nation's information technology architecture. A real-time understanding of threats and vulnerabilities is necessary for government officials and industry leaders to make decisions about tactical protective and response measures."); Kimberly Peretti, *Cyber Threat Intelligence: To Share or Not to Share—What Are the Real Concerns?,* 13 PVLR 1476 (2014) ("[T]he receipt of critical threat data can and has been shown to prevent potential cyberattacks and mitigate ongoing attacks."); Denise E. Zheng and James A. Lewis, *Cyber Threat Information Sharing: Recommendations for Congress and the Administration,* CTR. FOR STRATEGIC AND INT'L STUDIES 1 (March 2015), available online https://csis.org/files/ publication/150310_cyberthreatinfosharing.pdf ("Cyber threat information sharing.... is a critical step toward improving cyber defenses."). For arguments against the value of cyber-information sharing, *see* Paul Rosenzweig, *The Administration's Cyber Proposals—Information Sharing,* LAWFARE, (January 16, 2015), *available at* http://www.lawfareblog.com/2015/01/the-administrations-cyber-proposals-information-sharing/ ("Given all the strum and drang, the worst part about all of this is that it seems to me to be portending a big debate over something that won't matter that much. Most of the analysts I know are in pretty wide agreement that the most significant types of threats come from sophisticated actors who are creating and deploying novel cyber threats. For those sorts of new threats, no amount of information sharing is useful.").

[33] *See* Gregory T. Nojeim, *Cybersecurity and Freedom on the Internet,* 4 NAT'L SECURITY L. & POL'Y 119, 126 (2010) ("Although laws authorize such sharing of information, actual practice has been inadequate.") (hereinafter "NojeimCybersecurity"); *see also* Peretti, *supra* note 32, at 4 ("While an increasing number of companies are recognizing the benefits of sharing information regarding cyber threats, many remain wary.... "); *Exchanging Cyber Threat Intelligence: There Has to Be a Better Way,* PONEMON INSTITUTE, (April 2014), *available at* http://content.internetidentity.com/acton/attachment/8504/f-001b/1/-/-/-/-/Ponemon%20Study.pdf (hereinafter "Ponemon Institute—Threat Intelligence") ("71 percent of respondents say there has to be a better way to exchange threat information than what exists today.").

[34] Among these concerns include worries about compromising proprietary information, a desire to not aid competitors, losing customer goodwill, and reputational harms that may occur if an entity discloses details about a prior cyberattack. *See* Sales, *supra* note 26, at 1549; *see also* Derek E. Bambauer, *Ghost in the Network,* 162 U. PA. L. REV. 1011, 1046 (2014) ("Firms have significant incentives not to disclose breaches or attacks. Revealing lapses could have reputation-related market effects. Publicly traded companies ... suffer drops in share price immediately after revealing security breaches. Disclosing vulnerability information risks further dissemination (even if inadvertent) that could lead to additional attacks ... firms may not want to aid competitors either by reducing their information security costs or by protecting them from the same attack.").

[35] *See* Ponemon Institute—Threat Intelligence, *supra* note 33, at 3.

[36] *See, e.g., Cybersecurity: Enhancing Coordination to Protect the Financial Sector, Hearing Before Senate Committee on Banking, Housing, and Urban Affairs,* 113th Cong. (2013) (statement of Joseph M. Demarest, Assistant Director, Cyber Division, Federal Bureau of Investigation, *available at* http://www.fbi.gov/news/testimony/cyber-securityenhancing-coordination-to-protect-the-financial-sector ("The FBI worked closely with Department of Homeland Security (DHS) to issue Joint Indicator Bulletins (JIBs) to the U.S. banks, which included thousands of IP addresses that participated in the attacks. The U.S. banks used the IP addresses to better mitigate future incidents, thus helping to ensure their business operations could proceed with less interruption of service to their customers."); *see generally* Sales, *supra* note 26, at 1547 ("[T]he government's highly resourceful intelligence agencies are simply better than the private sector at detecting intrusions by sophisticated adversaries like foreign militaries and developing countermeasures. The government can provide these firms with the signatures of malware used in previous attacks, and firms can use the signature files to detect future intrusions.").

[37] *See, e.g., About Us: Information Sharing and Analysis Centers (ISACs),* NATIONAL COUNCIL OF ISACS, (no date provided), *available at* http://www.isaccouncil.org /aboutus.html.

[38] *See, e.g.,* Rachael King, *Cyber Attackers Target Building Management Systems,* WALL STREET JOURNAL, (April 5, 2013), *available at* http://blogs /cyber-attackers-target-building-management-systems/.

[39] The White House recently announced the creation of the Cyber Threat Intelligence Integration Center (CTIIC), an agency housed within the Office of the Director of National Intelligence (DNI) and will be modelled off of the National Counterterroism Center (NCTC) to share cyber-intelligence across various entities within the federal government. *See* The White House, *Presidential Memorandum—Establishment of the Cyber Threat Intelligence Integration Center,* (February 25, 2015), http://www.whitehouse.gov/the-press-office/2015 /02/25/presidential-memorandumestablishment-cyber-threat-intelligence-integrat.

[40] *See Stakeholder Priorities for the Quadrennial Homeland Security Review Hearing Before the Subcomm. on Oversight and Managment Efficiency of the H. Comm. on Homeland Security,* 113th Cong. (2014) (statement of Frank J. Cilluffo, Director Homeland Security Policy Institute and Cybersecurity Initiative The George Washington University) ("Currently responsibility for cyber analysis is split between the DHS Office of Intelligence and Analysis (I&A), and the National Protection and Programs Directorate.").

[41] *See* P.L. 107-296, Title II, Subtitle A, §201, codified at 6 U.S.C. §121(a). Under the Homeland Security Act of 2002, the term "terrorism" encompasses an act that is (1) "dangerous to human life or potentially destructive of critical infrastructure or key resources;" (2) a violation of federal or state or local criminal law; and (3) appears to be intended to either (a)

intimidate or coerce a civilian population, (b) influence the policy of a government by intimidation or coercion, or (c) affect the conduct of a government by mass destruction, assassination, or kidnapping. *See* 6 U.S.C. §101(16).

[42] 6 U.S.C. §121(d)(1).

[43] *Id.* §121(d)(1)(A)-(C).

[44] 6 U.S.C. §121(d)(3), (8), (13), (21).

[45] *Id.* §143(1)(A).

[46] *See* Perales v. Sullivan, 948 F.2d 1348, 1355 (2d Cir. 1991) ("Similar language in two different sections of the same law should be given a similar interpretation.") (citing Northcross v. Board of Education, 412 U.S. 427, 428 (1973) (*per curiam*))

[47] *See id.* §101(4) (citing 42 U.S.C. §5195c(e)) (defining "critical infrastructure," which includes both critical assets and systems).

[48] *See id.* §143(1)(A).

[49] *See Office of Intelligence and Analysis' Vision and Goals, Hearing Before the H. Comm. on Homeland Security,* 111th Cong. (2010) (statement of Under Secretary and Chief Intelligence Officer Caryn Wagner), *available at* http://www.dhs.gov/news/2010/05/12 /testimony-under-secretary-and-chief-intelligence-officer-caryn-wagner-andprincipal (" I&A also possesses a cyber intelligence analytic program. This team provides a national intelligence analytical framework in support of key cybersecurity customers, such as the DHS National Cybersecurity and Communications Integration Center (NCCIC), the DHS United States Computer Emergency Readiness Team (USCERT), and the Industrial Control Systems CERT. We are working with partners in the community to collaborate on strategic cyber analysis, and we continue to determine the amount of analytic support necessary to the Department's cybersecurity mission.").

[50] *See About the National Protection and Programs Directorate,* Dep't of Homeland Security, (July 9, 2014), *available at* http://www.dhs.gov/about-national-protection-and-programs-directorate.

[51] *See* Dep't of Homeland Sec. Appropriations Act, 2007, P.L. 109-295, Title VI, Subtitle A, §611(13), 120 Stat. 1409, *codified at* 6 U.S.C. §321c.

[52] *See About the National Protection and Programs Directorate,* Dep't of Homeland Security, (July 9, 2014), *available at* http://www.dhs.gov/about-national-protection-and-programs-directorate (describing the "mission" of CS&C).

[53] *See Facilitating Cyber Threat Information Sharing and Partnering with the Private Sector to Protect Critical Infrastructure: An Assessment of DHS Capabilities, Hearing Before Subcomm. on Cybersecurity, Infrastructure Protection and Security Technologies H. Comm. on Homeland Security,* 113th Cong. (2013) (statement of NPPD Office of CS&C Acting Assistant Secretary Roberta Stempfley and NCCIC Director Larry Zelvin) (hereinafter "Stempfley and Zelvin").

[54] *See* Press Release, *Secretary Napolitano Opens New National Cybersecurity and Communications Integration Center,* (October 30, 2009), *available at* http://www.dhs.gov/news/2009/10/30/new-national-cybersecurity-centeropened.

[55] *See* Stempfley and Zelvin, *supra* note 53.

[56] *See* Jason Miller, *DHS finds classified cyber sharing program slow to take off,* FEDERAL NEWS RADIO, (June 13, 2013), *available at* http://www.federalnewsradio.com/473 /3356694/DHS-finds-classified-cyber-sharing-program-slowto-take-off (distinguishing between ECS and CISCP based on the types of information shared with the private sector); *see also* Robert Gyenes, *A Voluntary Cybersecurity Framework Is Unworkable—Government Must Crack the Whip,* 14 PGH. J. Tech. L. & Pol'y 293, 305-06 (2014) (noting

that CISCP, because of its focus on sharing unclassified information, has a higher participation rate than ECS). President Obama's 2013 Executive Order on cybersecurity expanded efforts to disclose unclassified cybersecurity information, requiring the "timely production of unclassified reports of cyber threats to the U.S. homeland that identify a specific targeted entity." *See Improving Critical Infrastructure Cybersecurity,* Exec. Order No. 13,636, §4(a), 78 *Federal Register* 11,739, 11,740-41 (February 12, 2013).

[57] *See* Dep't of Homeland Sec., *Critical Infrastructure and Key Resources Cyber Information Sharing and Collaboration Program* 1, (no date provided), *available at* https://www.us-cert.gov/sites/default/files/c3vp/ CISCP_20140523.pdf. According to DHS, to join CISCP and gain access to NCCIC's cyber intelligence, a private entity must sign a Cooperative Research and Development Agreement (CRADA) with the agency. *Id.* Pursuant to the Stevenson-Wydler Technology Innovation Act of 1980, agencies are authorized to enter into CRDAs with private parties "under which the Government ... provides personnel, services, facilities, equipment, intellectual property, or other resources with or without reimbursement ... and the non-Federal parties provide funds, personnel, services, facilities, equipment, intellectual property, or other resources toward the conduct of specified research or development efforts which are consistent with the mission [of the agency]." *See* 15 U.S.C. §3710a(d)(1).

[58] *See* Dep't of Homeland Sec., *Enhanced Cybersecurity Services* 1, *available at* http://www.dhs.gov/sites/default/files/ publications/ECS-Fact-Sheet.pdf (emphasis added). The private entities that participate in ECS and receive government furnished threat indicators are either Commercial Service Providers (CSP) or Operational Implementers (OIs) who have been vetted by the government and entered into a Memorandum of Understanding with DHS. *See id.* at 2. CSPs, such as AT&T, provide information services to private entities, while an OI is a private entity who provides information services for its own network. *See* Defense Cyber Crime Center, *DIB Enhanced Cybersecurity Services (DECS),* (February 26, 2013), *available at* http://www.dc3.mil/data/uploads/dcise-pdf-dib-enhanced-cybersecurity-servicesprocedures_updated-feb-26-2013.pdf (describing the Department of Defense's precursor to ECS). Regardless, either a OI or CSP must be capable of implementing government furnished information, comply with applicable security requirements, and have appropriately cleared personnel and facilities in order to participate in ECS. *Id.* ECS was expanded pursuant to President Obama's 2013 Executive Order on cybersecurity. *See Improving Critical Infrastructure Cybersecurity,* Exec. Order No. 13,636, §4(c), 78 *Federal Register* 11,739, 11,740-41 (February 12, 2013) ("To assist the owners and operators of critical infrastructure in protecting their systems from unauthorized access, exploitation, or harm, the Secretary ... in collaboration with the Secretary of Defense, shall, within 120 days of the date of this order, establish procedures to expand the [ECS] program to all critical infrastructure sectors.") For more on the origins of ECS and the President's Executive Order, *see* CRS Report R42984, *The 2013 Cybersecurity Executive Order: Overview and Considerations for Congress*, by Eric A. Fischer et al., at pp. 10-11.

[59] P.L. 113-282, 128 Stat. 3066.

[60] 6 U.S.C. §148(c)(1). The Center is composed of various federal entities, such as sector-specific agencies, law enforcement agencies, and members of the intelligence community, and non-federal entities, such as state and local governments, information sharing and analysis organizations, and owners and operators of critical information systems. *Id.* §148(d).

[61] *Id.* §148(c).

[62] *Id.* §148(d)(1)(A)-(B).

[63] *Id.* §148(d)(1)(E).

[64] *See Executive Order, Promoting Private Sector Cybersecurity Information Sharing,* THE WHITE HOUSE, (February 13, 2015), §2(c), *available at* http://www.whitehouse.gov/the-press-office/2015/02/13/executive-order-promotingprivate-sector-cybersecurity-information-shari.

[65] 6 U.S.C. §131(5).

[66] *See, e.g.,* P.L. 107-296, Title II, Subtitle A, §201(d)(1) ("[T]he responsibilities of the Under Secretary for Information Analysis and Infrastructure Protection shall be ... to access, receive, and analyze law enforcement information, intelligence information, and other information from agencies of the Federal Government, State and local government agencies ... and private sector entities, and to integrate such information in order to ... identify and assess the nature and scope of terrorist threats to the homeland ... ").

[67] *Id.* §223 ("In carrying out the responsibilities under section 201, the Under Secretary for Information Analysis and Infrastructure Protection shall ... as appropriate, provide to State and local government entities, and upon request to private entities that own or operate critical information systems ... analysis and warnings related to threats to, and vulnerabilities of, critical information systems.").

[68] *See* 6 U.S.C. §148(c).

[69] *Id.*§148(a)(1) (defining "cybersecurity risk" to mean "threats to and vulnerabilities of information or information systems and any related consequences caused by or resulting from unauthorized access, use, disclosure, degradation, disruption, modification, or destruction of information or information systems, including such related consequences caused by an act of terrorism"); *see also id.* §148(a)(4) (citing 44 U.S.C. §3502(8) (defining "information system" to mean "a discrete set of information resources organized for the collection, processing, maintenance, use, sharing, dissemination, or disposition of information").

[70] 6 U.S.C. §148(d)(1)(E).

[71] *See* 42 U.S.C. §5195c(e) (defining "critical infrastructure," which includes both critical assets and systems).

[72] *See, e.g.,* Sean Lyngaas, *Can DHS get it together?,* FEDERAL COMPUTER WEEK, (October 31, 2014), *available at* http://fcw.com/articles/2014/10/31/cybersecurity-can-dhs-get-it-together.aspx (noting difficulty integrating threat analyses done by I&A with the work of NPPD); *see generally,* Paul Rosenzweig, *Cyber Security: A Complex 'Web' of Problems,* HERITAGE Foundation, (August 26, 2010), *available at* http://www.heritage.org /research/reports/2010/08/ cyber-security-a-complex-web-of-problems#_ftnref2 ("Today, as it pertains to cyber security, America still needs clearer lines of authority within the federal government and a more coherent structure of public–private interaction to allow for effective action.") (hereinafter "Rosenzweig-Heritage"); Robert Kenneth Palmer, *Critical Infrastructure: Legislative Factors for Preventing a "Cyber Pearl Harbor,"* 18 VA. J.L. & TECH. 289, 329 (2014) ("There are too many government agencies with different cyber-missions working independently, with project duplication to the point that it is not uncommon for several different groups to be working on the same thing, unaware of each other's efforts."); *but see Cybersecurity, Terrorism, and Beyond: Addressing Evolving Threats to the Homeland, Hearing Before S. Comm. on Homeland Security and Gov't Affairs,* 113th Cong (2014) (testimony of Under Secretary Francis Taylor and NPPD Under Secretary Suzanne Spaulding), *available at* http://www.dhs.gov/news/2014/09/10/written-testimony-ia-and-nppd-senate-committee-homeland-security-and-governmental ("I&A and NPPD work closely together every day to recognize and reduce risks posed by cyber

threats."). In this vein, some have lamented the fact that the disperse authorities respecting cyber-intelligence sharing have resulted in key entities, like US-CERT, lacking any specific authority to request cooperation from other agencies within DHS or the rest of the government on cyberintelligence efforts. *See Examining the Cyber Threat to Critical Infrastructure and the American Economy: Hearing before the H. Comm. of Homeland Security, Subcomm. on Cybersecurity, Infrastructure Protection, and Security Technologies*, 112th Cong. 50 (2011) (testimony of Mischel Kwon, President, Mischel Kwon & Associates, LLC), available at http://www.gpo.gov/fdsys/pkg/CHRG-112hhrg72221/pdf/CHRG-112hhrg72221.pdf ("US–CERT does not have the authority to require the departments or agencies to share detailed information, or follow any specific instructions"); *see also* Palmer, *supra* note 72, at 327 ("A significant part of the US-CERT's mission is to 'coordinate and collaborate' with critical infrastructure owners and operators, but this is rarely accomplished because the USCERT is buried within the DHS and has no authority to compel sector-specific federal agencies or law enforcement to coordinate and cooperate with the US-CERT's activities.").

[73] *See* 6 U.S.C. §121(d)(3)-(4).

[74] *See id.* §148(c)(2).

[75] *See supra* note 39.

[76] *See, e.g.*, Richard Bejtlich, *What are the prospects for the Cyber Threat Intelligence Integration Center?*, BROOKINGS INSTITUTION, (February 19, 2015), *available at* http://www.brookings.edu/blogs/techtank/posts/2015/02/19-cybersecurity-center-bejlich ("Some may view CTIIC as just the latest in a long line of cyber agencies created by the government ... The concern with CTIIC, however, is the perception that it duplicates the mission of NCCIC and older units.").

[77] The federal government is authorized to provide, without request, "analysis and warnings related to threats to, and vulnerabilities of, critical information systems" to state and local government entities. *See* 6 U.S.C. §143(1). Moreover, the Homeland Security Act authorizes DHS to make general recommendations and disseminate information analyzed by the Department as "appropriate" or "necessary." *See id.* §121(d)(6)-(8).

[78] *See id.* §143(1).

[79] *See* P.L. 113-282, §8, 128 Stat. 3072.

[80] *See* Broggi, *supra* note 31, at 658 ("On the contrary, the phrase 'upon request' suggests any such mandate is forbidden.").

[81] *See* Palmer, *supra* note 72, at 358 ("Even after two decades, voluntary information sharing has failed to create an effective information sharing environment.... ").

[82] 6 U.S.C. §121(d)(11)(A); *see also* 6 U.S.C. §141(2) (authorizing the Secretary of DHS to "establish procedures on the use of information shared under this title that ... ensure the security and confidentiality of such information.... ").

[83] *Id.* §121(d)(11)(B). For more information on the laws governing the protection of classified information, *see* CRS Report RS21900, *The Protection of Classified Information: The Legal Framework*, by Jennifer K. Elsea.

[84] *See* Gus P. Coldebella and Brian M. White, *Foundational Questions Regarding the Federal Role in Cybersecurity*, 4 J. NAT'L SEC. L. & POL'Y 233, 240-41 (2010) ("While the government has information about malicious code and the behavior of criminal networks gained through its intelligence and law enforcement functions, fears of botching investigations or compromising sources and methods make sharing with the private sector (or even with other government agencies) difficult.").

[85] *See* 6 U.S.C. §121(d)(14)(b); *see also* 6 U.S.C. §141(3) (authorizing the Secretary of DHS to "establish procedures on the use of information shared under this title that ... protect the constitutional and statutory rights of any individuals who are subjects of such information.... ").

[86] *See* 6 U.S.C. §148(e)(3).

[87] *See* 5 U.S.C. §552a(b) (generally prohibiting an agency from disclosing "any record which is contained in a system of records by any means of communication to any person, or to another agency.... "). Pursuant to the Privacy Act and the Homeland Security Act, DHS has promulgated Fair Information Practice Principles (FIPPs), which generally amount to framework for how the Department uses and disseminates information containing personal identifying information. *See* Hugo Teufel III, DHS Privacy Policy Guidance, DEP'T OF HOMELAND SEC., (December 29, 2008), *available at* http://www.dhs.gov/xlibrary/assets /privacy/privacy_policyguide_2008-01.pdf. However, it should be noted that the Privacy Act does contains exemptions for some inter-agency data sharing for national security and law enforcement purposes, as well as routine uses described by the agency in the Federal Register. *See* 5 U.S.C. §§552a(a)(8)(B)(vi), (b)(3), (b)(7), (e)(4)(D), & (j). There are numerous other more narrowly applicable laws on privacy and data protection that protect specific types of information in the possession of the government that could implicate the sharing of federal cyber-intelligence. *See, e.g.,* 42 U.S.C. §1320(d) & 45 C.F.R. §§160, 164 (Health Insurance Portability and Accountability Act of 1996); 18 U.S.C. §1905 (Trade Secrets Act).

[88] *See* Palmer, *supra* note 72, at 326.

[89] *Id.*

[90] *Id.* at 327.

[91] *See* Peretti, *supra* note 32, at 4 (noting concerns with current legal incentives governing private cyber-information sharing); *see also* Palmer, *supra* note 72, at 317-18 ("Although many of these limitations may be less limiting than they are perceived to be, the result of these perceptions and, at the very least, the uncertainty about the state of the law as they pertain to information sharing, have created collective inaction where individual companies often simply feel safer by keeping threat information to themselves rather than sharing it for mutual benefit."); CRS Report R43821, *Legislation to Facilitate Cybersecurity Information Sharing: Economic Analysis*, by N. Eric Weiss.

[92] *See* Peretti, *supra* note 32, at 2.

[93] *See* Ponemon Institute—Threat Intelligence, *supra* note 33, at 5 (noting that 58% of a survey's respondents rely on "peers in other companies" as their main source of threat intelligence).

[94] *See* Peretti, *supra* note 32, at 2.

[95] *See* Memorandum from President William Clinton on Critical Infrastructure Protection (Presidential Decision Directive/NSC-63) (May 22, 1998), *available at* http://www.fas.org/irp/offdocs/pdd/pdd-63.htm.

[96] *See* Peretti, *supra* note 32, at 4.

[97] 18 U.S.C. §§2510-2522.

[98] *Id.* §§2701-2711.

[99] *Id.* §§3121-3127.

[100] The Wiretap Act imposes significant criminal penalties on those who violate its terms, with a minimum of a ten thousand dollar fine per violation and up to five years of imprisonment. *See id.* §§2511, 2520.

[101] *Id.* §2520(a).

[102] *Id.* §2511(1)(a). Put another way, to show a violation of Title I of ECPA, five elements must be shown: the person or entity (1) intentionally (2) intercepted, endeavored to intercept or procured another person to intercept or endeavor to intercept (3) the contents of (4) an electronic communication (5) using a device. *See In re* Phramatrak Privacy Litig., 329 F.3d 9, 18 (1st Cir. 2003).

[103] An electronic communication includes any "transfer of signs, signals, writing, images, sounds, data, or intelligence of any nature transmitted in whole or in part by a wire, radio, electromagnetic, photoelectronic or photoptical system." *See* 18 U.S.C. §2510(12).

[104] 18 U.S.C. §2510(4) & (8). The statute also generally prohibits conduct related to or taken as a consequence of an illegal interception of covered communication, such as the use of a device to intercept a covered communication, the disclosure of illegally intercepted communications, or the use of illegally intercepted communications. *See* 18 U.S.C. §2511 (b)-(e).

[105] *See* Fraser v. Nationwide Mut. Ins. Co., 352 F.3d 107, 114 (3d Cir. 2003); Steve Jackson Games, Inc. v. U.S. Secret Serv., 36 F.3d 457, 462 (5th Cir. 1994); Konop v. Hawaiian Airlines, Inc., 302 F.3d 868, 878 (9th Cir. 2002); United States v. Steiger, 318 F.3d 1039, 1048-49 (11th Cir. 2003); *but see* United States v. Councilman 418 F.3d 67, 80 (1st Cir. 2005) (*en banc*) (suggesting that ECPA may not require "contemporaneity or real-time" transmission of electronic communications).

[106] *See* 18 U.S.C. §2511(3)(a).

[107] *See id.* §2511(1)(c)-(d).

[108] *See generally* Noel v. Hall, 568 F.3d 743, 749 (9th Cir. 2009) (holding that an interception of a covered communication "occurs 'when the contents of a ... communication are captured or redirected in any way.'") (quoting United States v. Rodriguez, 968 F.2d 130, 136 (2d Cir. 1992)); *see, e.g.* Campbell v. Facebook, Inc.,—F.Supp.3d—-, 2014 WL 7336475, at *3 (N.D.Cal. December 23, 2014) (holding the use of a software application to scan the content of private messages for marketing purposes amounts to "redirection" of the contents of the users' messages); *In re* Yahoo Mail Litig., 7 F. Supp. 3d 1016, 1027 (N.D. Cal. 2014) (holding that accessing the content of emails in transit constitutes an interception for purposes of ECPA).

[109] *See generally* Shubert v. Metrophone, Inc., 898 F.2d 401, 405 (3d Cir. 1990) (holding that §2511(3)(a) "prohibits a communication service provider from intentionally divulging the contents of a communication while in the transmission of that service.").

[110] *See* Broggi, *supra* note 31, at 661-62 ("[S]ignatures are comprised of indicators, and ... indicators may include text strings. If these strings are located in the body or subject line of an email, courts will consider them contents.").

[111] *See, e.g.,* Palmer, *supra* note 72, at 368 ("The nation needs real-time situational awareness and innovative cybersecurity standards to keep up with the technological curve of cyber-threats that confront critical infrastructure.").

[112] The Wiretap Act's prohibition on the use of a "device" to intercept any oral communication, *see* 18 U.S.C. §2511(b), contains another exception that may be relevant for those engaged in cyber-threat detection. Specifically, ECPA's definition of a "device" necessarily excludes "any device or apparatus" used by "any ... equipment or facility ... furnished to the subscriber or user ... in the ordinary course of business." *See id.* §2510(5)(a). However, the "ordinary course of business" exception may not apply to a private entity that is scanning electronic communication for potential cyber-threats. Courts have generally interpreted the ordinary course of business exemption to apply to devices that further an underlying communications system, such as routers or switchboards, which arguably is unrelated to

determining whether particular communications within such a system pose a cyber-threat. *See In re* Google Inc. Gmail Litigation, No. 13–MD–02430, 2013 WL 5423918, at *8 (N.D. Cal. September 26, 2013) (holding the "ordinary course of business exception" "offers protection from liability only where an electronic communication service provider's interception facilitates the transmission of the communication at issue or is incidental to the transmission of such communication. Specifically, the exception would apply here only if the alleged interceptions were an instrumental part of the transmission of email."); *see also Campbell,* 2014 WL 7336475, at *7 (holding the ordinary course of business exception requires some nexus between interception and the subscriber's "ultimate business, that is, the ability to provide the underlying service or good"); *see generally* Sanders v. Robert Bosch Corp., 38 F.3d 736, 740 (4th Cir. 1994) (refusing to apply the ordinary course of business exemption to a voice logger); Hall v. EarthLink Network, Inc., 396 F.3d 500, 504-5 (2d Cir. 2005); Williams v. Poulos, 11 F.3d 271, 280 (1st Cir. 1993); Deal v. Spears, 980 F.2d 1153, 1158 (8th Cir. 1992); *but see* Kirch v. Embarq Mgmt. Co., 702 F.3d 1245, 1250 (10th Cir. 2012) (holding that an Internet Service Provider was operating in the ordinary course of business by allowing an online advertising company to conduct technology tests for directing online advertising on electronic communications that the provider ordinary accessed). More broadly, courts have been reluctant to find that indiscriminate recording of communications is within the ordinary course of most businesses. *See, e.g.,* United States v. Murdock, 63 F.3d 1391, 1397 (6th Cir. 1995).

[113] *See* 18 U.S.C. §2511(2)(d); *id.* §2511(3)(b)(ii).

[114] *See* 18 U.S.C. §2511(2)(d); *id.* §2511(3)(b)(ii). In addition, under the consent exception to the Wiretap Act' s interception prohibition, the exception does not apply when the underlying communication is "intercepted for the purposes of committing any criminal or tortious act in violation of the Constitution or laws of the United States or of any State." *Id.* §2511(2)(d).

[115] *See* Gilday v. Dubois, 124 F.3d 277, 297 (1st Cir. 1997) (citing Griggs-Ryan v. Smith, 904 F.2d 112, 116 (1st Cir. 1990).

[116] *See* Dep't of Justice, *Searching and Seizing Computers and Obtaining Electronic Evidence in Criminal Investigations,* 172 (2009), *available at* http://www.justice.gov/criminal /cybercrime/docs/ssmanual2009.pdf.

[117] *See* Pitts Sales, Inc. v. King World Prods., 383 F. Supp. 2d 1354, 1361 (S.D. Fla. 2005) (holding that a "party to the communication" under §2511(2)(d) is a party "who is present when the ... communication is uttered and need not directly participate in the conversation"); *see also* United States v. Mullins, 992 F.2d 1472, 1478 (9th Cir. 1993) (stating that the consent exception of §2511(2)(d) authorizes monitoring of computer system misuse because the owner of the computer system is a party to the communication).

[118] *See generally* Brown v. Waddell, 50 F.3d 285, 289 (4th Cir. 1995); *see also* Orin Kerr, *Internet Surveillance Law After the USA PATRIOT Act: The Big Brother That Wasn't,* 97 NW. U. L. REV. 607, 620 (2003) 664-665 ("[L]abeling the [provider] a party to the communication may sound logical ... but ultimately would eviscerate the privacy protections of the Wiretap Act.").

[119] *See* Caro v. Weintraub, 618 F.3d 94, 97 (2d Cir. 2010) (holding that a "a party to the conversation is one who takes part in the conversation.").

[120] *See In re Pharmatrak Privacy Litig.*, 329 F.3d at 19 (citing Griggs-Ryan v. Smith, 904 F.2d 112, 119 (1st Cir. 1990)). Moreover, consent may be explicit or implied, but it must be actual consent rather than constructive consent. *Id.*

[121] United States v. Footman, 215 F.3d 145, 155 (1st Cir. 2000) ("The question of consent, either express or implied, may vary with the circumstances of the parties.").

[122] *See, e.g.*, Backhuat v. Apple, Inc.,—F.Supp.3d—, 2014 WL 6601776, at *8 (N.D. Cal. November 19, 2014) ("In light of the specific language of the license agreement, the Court concludes that a reasonable iMessage user would not be adequately notified that Apple would intercept his or her messages when doing so would not 'facilitate delivery' of the messages."); *In re Yahoo Mail Litig.*, 7 F.Supp.3d at 1029 ("The Court concludes that the [Yahoo Global Communications Additional Terms of Service for Yahoo Mail and Yahoo Messenger] establishes explicit consent by Yahoo Mail users to Yahoo's conduct."); *In re Google Inc. Gmail Litig.*, 2013 WL 5423918, at *11–14 ("[A] reasonable Gmail user who read the Privacy Policies would not have necessarily understood that her emails were being intercepted to create user profiles or to provide targeted advertisements. Accordingly, the Court finds that it cannot conclude at this phase that the new policies demonstrate that Gmail user Plaintiffs consented to the interceptions.").

[123] *See Griggs-Ryan,* 904 F.2d at 117-18.

[124] *See Berry v. Funk,* 146 F.3d 1003, 1011 (D.C. Cir. 1998).

[125] *See Watkins v. L.M. Berry & Co.*, 704 F.2d 577, 581 (11th Cir. 1983).

[126] *See In re Pharmatrak Inc.*, 329 F.3d at 20.

[127] *See* 18 U.S.C. §2511(2)(a)(i). The provider exception also contains a provision that allows the service provider to intercept, disclose, or use cover communications when the activity is a necessary incident to the rendition of a service. *Id.* This exception generally allows interception that is "unavoidable" and a part and parcel of modern telecommunications. U.S. Dep't of Justice, *supra* note 116, at 177 (citing United States v. New York Tel. Co., 434 U.S. 159, 168 n.13 (1977)).

[128] *See* 18 U.S.C. §2511(2)(a)(i).

[129] *See, e.g.,* United States v. Pervaz, 118 F.3d 1, 5 (1st Cir. 1997) (holding that a company had the right to intercept covered communications where there was evidence that its customers were being defrauded); *see generally* United States v. Harvey, 540 F.2d 1345, 1352 (8th Cir. 1976) ("18 U.S.C. §2511(2)(a)(i) ... was designed to allow the disclosure of justified wire monitoring" in order to provide evidence for "wire fraud prosecution"); *New York Tel. Co.*, 434 U.S. at 168 n.13 (stating in *dicta* that the provider exception "excludes all normal telephone company business practices from the prohibitions of the [Wiretap] Act.").

[130] *See* United States v. Mullins, 992 F.2d 1472, 1478 (9th Cir. 1993) (holding that an employee of an electronic communication service can act to "protect the rights and property of her employer by monitoring ... apparent misuse of [the] electronic communication service."); Campiti v. Walonis, 611 F.2d 387, 393 (1st Cir. 1979) ("The section is obviously intended to allow the telephone company to intercept and disclose calls as a necessary protection of *its* equipment and rights") (emphasis added); United States v. Auler, 539 F.2d 642, 646 (7th Cir. 1976) (holding that telephone companies which intercept calls pursuant to §2511(2)(a)(i) may forward to the police no more of the content of those calls than "necessary to protect company rights and property."); Hodge v. Mountain States Tel. & Tel. Co., 555 F.2d 254, 260 (9th Cir. 1977) ("Congress enacted §2511(2)(a)(i) 'to reflect existing law' which allowed telephone companies to intercept communications in order to protect the *integrity* of their property.") (emphasis added).

[131] *See Legal Issues Relating to the Testing, Use, & Deployment of an Intrusion-Detection Sys. (Einstein 2.0) to Protect Unclassified Computer Networks in the Exec. Branch,* 33 OP. O.L.C. 1 (2009).

[132] *See* Broggi, *supra* note 31, at 669-70; *see also Protecting America From Cyber Attacks: the Importance of Information Sharing, Hearing Before the Senate Homeland Security and Gov't Affairs Committee,* (January 28, 2015), statement of Gregory T. Nojeim, Senior Counsel and Director of the Freedom, Security and Technology Project, at pg. 5, *available at* https://d1ovv0c9tw0h0c.cloudfront.net/files/2015/01/HSGAC-Cybersec-tes-1-28-15-final-TEH.pdf (hereinafter "Nojeim Testimony").

[133] The Wiretap Act does have other means for the *government* to intercept or receive electronic communications. *See, e.g.,* 18 U.S.C. §§2516-2518 (authorizing government access to covered communications pursuant to or in anticipation of a court order); *id.* §2511(2)(i) (permitting "a person acting under color of law" to "intercept" the contents of "wire or electronic communications of a computer trespasser transmitted to, through, or from [a] protected computer" under limited circumstances).

[134] *See* Aaron J. Burstein, *Amending the ECPA to Enable a Culture of Cybersecurity Research,* 22 HARV. J.L. & TECH. 167, 188 (2008) ("Even if a researcher intercepts electronic communications contents under the provider exception, disclosing the contents to *outside* researchers might stretch the requirement of protecting the original service provider's rights or property.") (emphasis added). Moreover, even if a provider, in collecting and sharing cyber-threat information, is ostensibly acting out of self-interest, courts have been clear that ECPA, by permitting interceptions to "protect the rights or property" of the provider, does not allow "unlimited" interceptions. *See Auler,* 539 F.2d at 646 (holding that the authority of a service provider to intercept and disclose covered communications is "not unlimited"); *Councilman,* 418 F.3d at 82 (holding that it was "indisputable" that the "narrow[]" provider exception did not exempt a provider who intercepted and copy all incoming communications to gain a commercial advantage). Instead, there must be a "substantial nexus" between the monitoring and the threat to the provider's rights or property. *See* United States v. McLaren, 957 F. Supp. 215, 219 (M.D. Fla. 1997). The Department of Justice has interpreted the provider exception to permit "providers and their agents to conduct reasonable monitoring that balances the providers' needs to protect their rights and property with their subscribers' right to privacy." *See* U.S. Dep't of Justice, *supra* note 116, at 173. At least one commentator has suggested that the substantial nexus test may limit the scope of what types of information can be gathered to combat cyber-threats. *See* Burstein, *supra* note 134, at 187 ("Although cybersecurity researchers might ... provide information that allows their employers to protect their networks, this connection is likely to be highly attenuated ... since researchers usually develop methods of detecting malicious traffic, their results might not be immediately applicable to that purpose.").

[135] *See* 18 U.S.C. §§2701-2702. What sorts of "storage" that the SCA regulates will depend several statutory terms that will be explained in more detail *infra.*

[136] The SCA also prohibits unauthorized access to an ECS facility and "thereby obtains, alters, or prevents authorized access to [an] ... electronic communication while it is in electronic storage.... " *See* 18 U.S.C. §2701(a). However, Section 2701 exempts from that general prohibition "conduct authorized ... by the person or entity providing [an] ... electronic communications service," *see id.* §2701(c)(1), meaning that service providers that "obtain" electronic communication while in storage for the purpose of determining cyber-threats are likely immune from liability under the first prohibition in the SCA. *See* Fraser v. Nationwide Mut. Ins. Co., 352 F.3d 107, 115 (3d Cir. 2003) ("[W]e read §2701(c) literally to except from Title II's protection all searches by communications service providers ... because Fraser's email was stored on Nationwide's system (which Nationwide administered), its search of that email falls within §2701(c)'s exception to Title II."); *see*

also In re Yahoo Mail Litig., 7 F. Supp. 3d at 1026-27 ("The SCA grants immunity to 18 U.S.C. §2701(a) claims to [ECS providers] for accessing content on their own servers."); Crowley v. Cybersource Corp., 166 F. Supp. 2d 1263, 1272 (N.D. Cal. 2001) (holding that ECS "could not have limited access to its own facilities."); *see generally Councilman,* 418 F.3d at 82 (noting the "breadth" of §2701(c)(1)'s provider exception).

[137] 18 U.S.C. §2702 prohibits what service providers can divulge with respect to *non-content* information only as it relates to disclosures made to the government. *See id.* §2702(a)(3). For a discussion of §2702(a)(3), *see infra* "Privacy Concerns."

[138] *See* 18 U.S.C. §2702(a)(1)-(2).

[139] *See* 18 U.S.C. §2702(b)-(c) (including in the civil relief for a violation of the SCA (1) equitable relief; (2) actual damages or at least $1,000; (3) punitive damages for willful or intentional conduct; (4) attorney fees).

[140] United States v. Smith, 155 F.3d 1051, 1055 (9th Cir. 1998) (describing the SCA as a "complex, often convoluted, area of the law.").

[141] 18 U.S.C. §2510(15).

[142] *See, e.g.,* Quon v. Arch Wireless Operating Co., Inc., 529 F.3d 892, 902 (9th Cir. 2008), *rev'd on other grounds by* City of Ontario v. Quon, 560 U.S. 746 (2010).

[143] *See, e.g.,* Theofel v. Farey-Jones, 359 F.3d 1066, 1075 (9th Cir. 2004).

[144] *Id.* §2711(2). In turn, an electronic communication system is "any wire, radio, electromagnetic, photoptical or photo electronic facilities for the transmission of wire or electronic communications, and any comput facilities or rleated electronic equipment for the electronic storage of such communications." *Id.* §2510(14).

[145] *See Quon,* 529 F.3d at 901.

[146] 18 U.S.C. §2702(a)(1).

[147] *See, e.g., In re* Zynga Privacy Litig., 750 F.3d 1098, 1108 (9th Cir. 2014) (noting that "email and IP addresses 'constitute addressing information and do not necessarily reveal any more about the underlying contents of communication than do phone numbers.'") (internal citations omitted).

[148] 18 U.S.C. §2702(a)(1).

[149] 18 U.S.C. §2710(17)(A)-(B).

[150] *See Theofel,* 359 F.3d at 1076.

[151] *See* Crispin v. Christian Audigier, Inc., 717 F. Supp. 2d 965, 987 (C.D. Cal. 2010); United States v. Weaver, 636 F. Supp. 2d 769, 771-73 (C.D. Ill. 2009); *see generally* Orin S. Kerr, *A User's Guide to the Stored Communications Act, and a Legislator's Guide to Amending It*, 72 GEO. WASH. L. REV. 1208, 1216-18 (2004) (explaining that emails that are in transit or have been delivered but are unopened are in electronic storage by an ECS, while emails that have been opened and saved exclusively on a server are stored in RCS) (hereinafter "Kerr-Guide").

[152] 18 U.S.C. §2702(a)(2)(A)-(B).

[153] *Id.* §2702(a)(2)(B); *see also* Viacom Int'l Inc. v. YouTube Inc., 253 F.R.D. 256, 264 n.8 (S.D.N.Y. 2008); Juror Number One v. Superior Court, 206 Cal. App. 4th 854, 862 ("Thus, if the service *is* authorized to access the customer's information for other purposes, such as to provide targeted advertising, SCA protection may be lost.").

[154] 18 U.S.C. §2702(a)(1)-(2).

[155] *See* Kerr-Guide, *supra* note 151, at 1229-33; *see also In re* Application of the United States of America for a Search Warrant for Contents of Electronic Mail and for an Order Directing a Provider of Electronic Communication Services to not Disclose the Existence of the Search Warrant, 665 F. Supp. 2d 1210, 1214 (D. Or. 2009) ("Today, most ISPs provide both ECS

and RCS; thus, the distinction serves to define the service that is being provided at a particular time (or as to a particular piece of electronic communication at a particular time), rather than to define the service provider itself.").

[156] *See Smith*, 155 F.3d at 1055.

[157] *See* Burstein, *supra* note 134, at 189; *see also infra* note 401 (discussing potential litigation costs).

[158] *Id.*

[159] Besides the other exceptions mentioned in this paragraph, under the SCA's exceptions to the prohibition in 18 U.S.C. §2702(a)(1)-(2), providers may divulge the contents of a communication to another private party to the extent the disclosure is made: (1) to the addressee or intended recipient of such communication, *id* §2702(b)(1), or (2) to the National Center for Missing and Exploited Children as required by federal statutes intended to prevent sexual exploitation or trafficking of children or criminalize the possession, creation, or transportation of child pornography, *id.* §§2702(b)(6), 2252A.

[160] *See* 18 U.S.C. §2702(b).

[161] *Id.* §2702(b)(4)

[162] *See* Burstein, *supra* note 134, at 189.

[163] *See* 18 U.S.C. §2702(b)(3) ("A provider ... may divulge the contents of a communication ... with the lawful consent of the originator or an address or intended recipient of such communication, or the subscriber in the case of [RCS].")

[164] *Compare* Bower v. Mirvat El-Nady Bower, 808 F. Supp. 2d 348, 351 (D. Mass. 2011) (finding no consent); *with* Flagg v. City of Detroit, 252 F.R.D. 346, 364 (E.D. Mich. 2008) (finding consent).

[165] *See Theofel,* 359 F.3d at 1076; *Quon,* 529 F.3d at 901-02; *see generally* Kerr-Guide, *supra* note 151, at 1215-16 ("The classifications of ECS and RCS are context sensitive: the key is the provider's role with respect to a particular copy of a particular communication, rather than the provider's status in the abstract. A provider can act as an RCS with respect to some communications, an ECS with respect to other communications, and neither an RCS nor an ECS with respect to other communications.").

[166] *See* 18 U.S.C. §2702(b)(5) ("A provider ... may divulge the contents of a communication ... as may be necessarily incident to the rendition of the service or to the protection of the rights or property of the provider of that service.") (emphasis added).

[167] *See* Burstein, *supra* note 134, at 190; *see also supra* note 133 (discussing the "substantial nexus" test).

[168] 18 U.S.C. §§3121-3127.

[169] *See* Burstein, *supra* note 134, at 191.

[170] *See* Daniel J. Solove, *Reconstructing Electronic Surveillance Law,* 72 GEO. WASH. L. REV. 1264, 1287 (2004) (contending that "e-mail headers (the addressing information on e-mail messages), IP addresses, and Uniform Resource Locators ... fall under [the] definition [of information captured by a pen/trap device]."); *see also* Dep't of Justice, *supra* note 116, at 154 ("Because Internet headers contain both 'to' and 'from' information, a device that reads the entire header ... is both a pen register and trap and trace device.... ").

[171] 18 U.S.C. §3121(a). Specifically, in relevant part, the Pen/Trap statute defines a "pen register" as a device that records or captures information that is "reasonably likely to identify the source of [an] ... electronic communication," *see id.* §3127(3), whereas a "trap and trace device" is defined as one that captures incoming electronic or other impulses that "identify the originating number or other dialing, routing, addressing, and signaling information reasonably likely to identify the source of [an] ... electronic communication," *id.* §3127(4).

Both definitions exclude devices that capture content information, *id.*§3127(3)-(4), and the definition for a pen register excludes "any device ... used by a provider or customer of [an] ... electronic communication service for billing, or recording as an incident to billing ... or any device ... used ... for cost accounting or other like purposes in the ordinary course of business," *id.*§3127(4).

[172] *See id.*§3121(d).

[173] 18 U.S.C. §3121(b)(1).

[174] *Id.* §3121(b)(3). The government can obtain authority to install a pen/trap device by certifying to a court "that the information likely to be obtained [from a pen register] is relevant to an ongoing criminal investigation" being conducted by a law enforcement agency. *See* 18 U.S.C. §3122(b).

[175] *Cf.* United States v. Reed, 575 F.3d 900, 914 (9th Cir. 2009) (concluding that the Pen/Trap Act contains no requirement that non-content information form a pen/trap device be sealed from public disclosure); *see* Burstein, *supra* note 134, at 192 ("The Pen/Trap statute's exception, however, si concerned only with the condition for allowing a service provider to install a pen register; the statute lacks a corresponding disclosure provision."); *see also* Broggi, *supra* note 31, at 672 ("Unlike the Wiretap Act however, the statute is silent regarding voluntary disclosure of information obtained under these exceptions.").

[176] 18 U.S.C. §3121(b)(1).

[177] *See* David D. Clark and Susan Landau, *Untangling Attribution*, 2 HARV. NAT'L SEC. J. 531, 534-35 (2011) (describing all "data transport service of the Internet" as being based on packets, "small units of data prefixed with delivery instructions.").

[178] *See* Columbia Pictures Industries v. Bunnell, No. 06-1093FMCJCX, 2007 WL 2080419, at *11 (C.D. Cal. May, 29, 2007 (holding that the capturing of an IP address necessary to "operate [a] website" falls within the Pen/Trap Act's provider exception).

[179] 18 U.S.C. §3121(b)(1).

[180] *See* Broggi, *supra* note 31, at 672 ("The purpose of using signatures to scan network traffic is to protect the network and its users from malicious activity.").

[181] 18 U.S.C. §3121(b)(3).

[182] There could be an argument that sharing non-content information with the *government* raises liability issues under the SCA. *See infra* "Privacy Concerns." Nonetheless, neither the SCA nor the Pen/Trap Act provide for criminal or civil liability when a private entity discloses non-content information to another private entity.

[183] *See generally* Omer Tenne, *Quantifying Harm Structure: A New Harm Matrix for Cybersecurity Surveillance,* 12 J. ON TELECOMM. & HIGH TECH. L. 391, 393-95 (2014) (discussing the key "legal distinctions that serve as proxies for the measurement of privacy and civil liberties harms.").

[184] The CCPA defines cable operators as:

> any person or group of persons (A) who provides cable service over a cable system and directly or through one or more affiliates owns a significant interest in such cable system, or (B) who otherwise controls or is responsible for, through any arrangement, the management and operation of such a cable system.

47 U.S.C. §522(5).

[185] 47 U.S.C. §551(b)(1) & (c)(1). The statute does not define the term of art "personally identifiable information," but does exclude from the term "any record of aggregate data which does not identify particular persons." *Id.* §551(a)(2)(A). Nonetheless, courts have recognized the term to include "specific information about the subscriber, or a list of names and addresses on which the subscriber is included.... " *See* Scofield v. Telecable of

Overland Park, Inc., 973 F.2d 874, 876 n. 2 (10th Cir.1992). Another court has held that a person's name, address, and telephone are included in term "personal identifiable information." *See* Warner v. Am. Cablevision of Kansas City, Inc. ., 699 F.Supp. 851, 855 (D.Kan.1988); *see also* Pruitt v. Comcast Cable Holdings, LLC, 100 Fed. App'x. 713, 716 (10th Cir.2004) (holding that a cable box did not contain PII where, *inter alia*, it did not contain the name, address, or "any other information regarding the customer."). There are several exceptions to the CCPA's general prohibition on collecting or disclosing PII, including a consent exception, *see* 47 U.S.C. §551(b)(1) & (c)(1), an exception based on the need to conduct a "legitimate business activity," *id.* §551(b)(2) & (c)(2), and an exception for disclosure to the government based on a court order, *id.*§551(c)(2)(B).

186 *Id.* §551(f) (allowing for liquidated damages calculated at a rate $100 for each day of a violation and punitive damages).

187 *See* Digital Sin, Inc. v. Does 1-176, 279 F.R.D. 239, 241 (S.D.N.Y. 2012) (finding that "many ... ISPs ... qualify as 'cable operators' under the CPPA and subject to the restrictions found in 47 U.S.C. §551); *see also* Warner Bros. Record Inc. v. Doe, 555 F. Supp. 2d 1, 2 (D.D.C. 2008) (ordering a subpoena to be issued upon a cable ISP under 47 U.S.C. §551(c)(2)); TCYK, Inc. v. Does 1-20, No. 3:13–cv–3927–L, 2013 WL 6475040, at *2 (N.D. Tex. December 10, 2014) ("The Cable Privacy Act prohibits cable operators, which includes the ISPs identified here, from disclosing subscribers' personal information without their consent or a court order."); AF Holdings LLC v. Doe, No. 12cv1519– BTM, 2012 WL 3238023, at *1-3 (S.D. Cal. January 29, 2013) (issuing an order under the CCPA for Cox Communications to produce "produce documents and information sufficient to identify the user of the specified IP address."); *see generally* United States v. Kennedy, 81 F. Supp. 2d 1103, 1111 (D. Kan. 2000) (assuming without holding that the CCPA applies to a "provider of high speed Internet services over cable wires"); *but see* Klimas v. Comcast Cable Communs., Inc., 465 F.3d 271, 273 (6th Cir. 2006) (holding that the CCPA's prohibition on the collection and dissemination of PII did not extend cable providers that also functioned as ISPs).

188 *See* 15 U.S.C. §§1681, *et seq.* (Fair Credit Reporting Act).

189 *See id.* §§6501-6506 (Children's Online Privacy Protection Act).

190 *See id.* §§6801-6809 (Gramm-Leach-Bliley Act (GLBA)).

191 *See* 18 U.S.C. §2710 (The Video Privacy Protection Act).

192 *See* 20 U.S.C. §1232g (Family Educational Rights and Privacy Act).

193 *See* 42 U.S.C. §300gg, 29 U.S.C §§1181 *et seq.*, 42 U.S.C. §§1320d *et seq.*, 45 C.F.R. Part 160 and Part 164, Subparts A and E (Health Insurance Portability and Accountability Act (HIPAA)).

194 *See* 47 U.S.C. §222 (Federal Communications Act). Section 222 could take on an important role with respect to ISPs, who may be the primary entities interested in engaging in cyber-information sharing, depending on whether such entities are considered a "common carrier" for purposes of Title II of the Communications Act and on whether the Federal Communications Commission promulgates new rules regarding how ISPs should protect customer proprietary network information under Section 222. *See* Press Release, *FCC Adopts Strong, Sustainable Rules to Protect Open Internet,* Federal Communications Commission, (February 26, 2015), at pg. 4, *available at* http://transition.fcc.gov/Daily_Releases/Daily_Business/2015/db0226/DOC-332260A1.pdf (noting that, under newly proposed net-neutrality rules, Section 222 of the Communications Act will apply to ISP); *see also In the Matter of* Protecting and Promoting the Open Internet, GN Docket No. 14-28, 53-54, 462-467 (F.C.C. February 26, 2015), *available at*

http://transition.fcc.gov/Daily_Releases/Daily_Business/2015/db0312/FCC-15-24A1.pdf (contemplating a "separate rulemaking procedure" for imposing customer privacy rules respecting ISPs).

[195] *See* CRS Report R41734, *Privacy: An Abridged Overview of the Electronic Communications Privacy Act*, by Charles Doyle, at p. 81 ("Appendix A"). Vermont is the only state that has not adopted its own state wiretapping statute. *Id.*

[196] *Id.*

[197] *See* Elisabeth Pride, *Down the Rabbit's Hole: Baby Monitors, Family Movies and Wiretap Law,* 23 J. AM. ACAD. MATRIMONIAL LAW. 131, 149 (2010) ("Generally speaking, the state wiretap laws are modeled on the federal Act and substantially mirror its language, but may be more restrictive in many respects.... "); *see also* Daniel R. Dinger, *Should Parents Be Allowed to Record a Child's Telephone Conversations When They Believe the Child Is in Danger?: An Examination of the Federal Wiretap Statute and the Doctrine of Vicarious Consent in the Context of a Criminal Prosecution,* 28 Seattle U.L. Rev. 955, 965-67 & n.58 (2005) (discussing the differing state wiretap laws).

[198] *See* Cal. Penal Code §632.7; Fla. Stat. Ann. §934.03; Ill. Comp. Stat. Ann. ch. 720 §§5/14-2—5/14-3; Md. Cts. §Jud. Pro. Code. Ann. §10-402(c)(3); Mich. Comp. Laws. Ann. §750.539c; Mont. Code. Ann. §§45-8-213; Ore. Rev. Stat. §165.540(c); Pa. Stat. Ann. tit. 13 §1504.

[199] *See* Bipartisan Policy Center, *supra* note 28, at 11.

[200] *See, e.g.,* Minn. Stat. §325M.02.(Minnesota's Internet Privacy Act) (generally prohibiting ISPs from "knowingly disclose a consumer's 'personally identifiable information.'").

[201] *See* Palmer, *supra* note 72, at 318; *see also* Peretti, *supra* note 32, at 5.

[202] *See* Ponemon Institute—Threat Intelligence, *supra* note 33, at 4; *see generally* Sales, *supra* note 26, at 1530 (finding that antitrust "liability fears appear to be fairly widespread" amongst firms that may wish "to share information or to adopt common security standards.").

[203] *See id.* at 1528-29. Several federal laws have prohibitions on anticompetitive behavior, including the Sherman Act, *see* 15 U.S.C. §§1-7, the Wilson Tariff Act, *id.* §§8-11, the Clayton Act, *id.* §§12-27, and the Federal Trade Commission Act, *id.* §45.

[204] *In re* Flonase Antitrust Litig., 692 F. Supp. 2d 524, 539 (E.D. Pa. 2010).

[205] *See* 15 U.S.C. §1.

[206] Board of Trade of Chicago v. United States, 246 U.S. 231, 238, 38 S. Ct. 242, 62 L. Ed. 683 (1918) (reasoning that the term "restraint of trade" in §1 cannot possibly refer to any restraint on competition because "[e]very agreement concerning trade, every regulation of trade, restrains. To bind, to restrain, is of their very essence").

[207] Copperweld Corp. v. Independence Tube Corp., 467 U.S. 752, 768 (1984).

[208] *Id.*; *see also* Nat'l Collegiate Athletic Ass'n v. Bd. of Regents of Univ. of Okla., 468 U.S. 85, 103-04 (1984) ("*Per se* rules are invoked when surrounding circumstances make the likelihood of anticompetitive conduct so great as to render unjustified further examination of the challenged conduct."); United States v. Socony-Vacuum Oil Co., 310 U.S. 150, 223 (1940) ("[C]ombination[s] formed for the purpose and with the effect of raising, depressing, fixing, pegging, or stabilizing the price of a commodity in interstate or foreign commerce is illegal *per se*.").

[209] *See Copperweld Corp.*, 467 U.S. at 768; *see generally Board of Trade,* 246 U.S. at 238 ("[T]he court must ordinarily consider the facts peculiar to the business to which the restraint is applied; its condition before and after the restraint was imposed; the nature of the restraint and its effect, actual or probable. The history of the restraint, the evil believed to

exist, the reason for adopting the particular remedy, the purpose or end sought to be attained, are all relevant facts.").

[210] *See* Ken Heyer, *A World of Uncertainty: Economics and Globalization of Antitrust,* 72 ANTITRUST L.J. 375, 378 (2005) (arguing that "antitrust analysis and decisionmaking" entails "considerable uncertainty and imprecision surrounding particular case decisions.").

[211] *See* 15 U.S.C. §1 (subjecting those guilty of violating §1 to fines "not exceeding $ 100,000,000 if a corporation, or, if any other person, $ 1,000,000," and "imprisonment not exceeding 10 years.... ").

[212] *Id.*§15a.

[213] *Id.*§15c.

[214] *Id.* §15.

[215] *Id.* §15(a) ("[A]ny person who shall be injured in his business or property by reason of anything forbidden in the antitrust laws ... shall recover threefold the damages by him sustained.... ").

[216] *See, e.g.,* Info. Tech Industry Council, *ITI Recommendation: Addressing Liability Concerns Impeding More Effective Cybersecurity Information Sharing* 3 (2012), *available at* http://www.itic.org/dotAsset/fae2feab-7b0e-45f4- 9e74-64e4c9ece132.pdf (suggesting that the if a company "voluntarily reports what may be a cybersecurity threat or incident in an information sharing entity, such as an ISAC," that includes competitors of the company, a "[p]otential result" would be for a "plaintiff [to] claim[] that the information shared is an effort to harm competition," resulting in a lawsuit under federal antitrust laws).

[217] *See* Dep't of Justice and Fed. Trade Comm'n, *Antitrust Policy Statement on Sharing of Cybersecurity Information* 8 (April 10, 2014), *available at* http://www.justice.gov/atr/public /guidelines/305027.pdf (hereinafter "DOJ-FTC Joint Statement") (noting that any antitrust analysis of a given cyber information sharing scheme is "intensely fact-driven.").

[218] *See* United States v. United States Gypsum Co., 438 U.S. 422, 443 n.16 (1978).

[219] *See* FTC v. Indiana Federation of Dentists, 476 U.S. 447, 458 (1986).

[220] *See* Sales, note 26, at 1531.

[221] *See id.* ("Whether the companies have agreed to purchase and install new firewall software ... industry members ... might decide to pass on these costs to consumer, either in the form of a general price hike or as free standing surcharge."); *see generally* United States v. Container Corp. of Am., 393 U.S. 333, 338 n.4 (1969) ("[A]ll forms of price-fixing are per se violations of the Sherman Act.").

[222] Sales, note 26, at 1531-32 ("Suppose firms in a particular industry agree to install intrusion-detection or –prevention capabilities to scan for malware ... [t]he effect [of which] is often to slow down the network's performance ... [T]he shared security standards still plausibly could be described as an unlawful price-fixing agreement ... [because] the firms have agree to require consumers to pay the *same* price for a *lesser* product.... ").

[223] *Id.* at 1531.

[224] *See United States Gypsum Co.*, 438 U.S. at 443 n.16; *see also* Augusta News Co. v. Hudson News Co., 269 F.3d 41, 47 (1st Cir. 2001) ("[T]he legality of *most* kinds of agreements (*e.g.*, R&D projects, information sharing, distribution contracts) is tested by the rule of reason.").

[225] Paladin Assocs. v. Montana Power Co., 328 F.3d 1145, 1156 (9th Cir. 2003).

[226] *Cf.* Michelman v. Clark-Schwebel Fiber Glass Corp., 534 F.2d 1036, 1048 (2d Cir. 1976) (holding that the concerted exchange of credit information was "necessary to protect ... against" fraud and, therefore, did not amount to "violation of §1 ... provided that any action taken in reliance upon [such information was] the result of each firm's independent judgment.... ").

[227] *Cf.* Reg'l Multiple Listing Serv. of Minn., Inc. v. Am. Home Realty Network, Inc., 9 F. Supp. 3d 1032, 1039 (D. Minn. 2014) (holding that an allegation that several real estate agents colluded in creating an information sharing network to exclude another broker sufficed to satisfy a Sherman Act §1 claim).

[228] *See* DOJ-FTC Joint Statement, *supra* note 217.

[229] *Id.* at 5.

[230] *Id.* at 6.

[231] *Id.* at 7-8.

[232] *Id.* at 4.

[233] *Id.* at 8.

[234] *Cf.* FTC v. Acavis, Inc. 133 S. Ct. 2223, 2245 (Roberts, C.J., dissenting) (describing the rule of reason as "unruly").

[235] The DOJ has developed a business review procedure, whereby groups can submit a specific plan to collaborate on cybersecurity efforts to the Justice Department for a determination by the agency of whether the proposed collaboration would raise antitrust concerns. *See* 28 C.F.R. §50.6; *see, e.g.,* Letter from Joel I. Klein, Assistant Attorney General, Dep't of Justice, Antitrust Div., to Barbara Greenspan, Assoc. Gen. Counsel, Elec. Power Research Inst., Inc. (October 2, 2000), *available at* http://justice.gov/atr/public/busreview/6614.htm.

[236] 15 U.S.C. §15(a).

[237] In order to succeed on such a claim, in addition to demonstrating a violation of federal antitrust law, a private party would have demonstrate an "antitrust injury"—i.e., that it possesses "antitrust standing"—which requires a showing that the plaintiff was harmed by the defendant's anticompetitive contract combination, or conspiracy, and that harm flowed from an "anti-competitive aspect of the practice under scrutiny." Atl. Richfield Co. v. USA Petroleum Co., 495 U.S. 328, 334 (1990).

[238] *See, e.g.,* Eric Engleman, *Companies Want Lawsuit Shield to Share Cyber Threat Data,* BLOOMBERG BUS. WK. (March 7, 2013), http://www.businessweek.com/news/2013-03-07/companies-want-lawsuit-shield-to-share-cyberthreat-data ("Companies are concerned about ... negligence lawsuits for failing to act on information they receive.... ").

[239] *See* Nat'l Research Council, CRITICAL INFORMATION INFRASTRUCTURE PROTECTION AND THE LAW: AN OVERVIEW OF KEY ISSUES 45-46 (Stewart D. Personick & Cynthia A. Patterson eds., 2003).

[240] *Id.* at 45.

[241] *See* Baidu, Inc. v. Register.com, Inc., 760 F. Supp. 2d 312, 320 (S.D.N.Y. 2010).

[242] *See, e.g.,* Citizens Bank of Pa. v. Reimbursement Techs., Inc., No. 12–1169, 2014 WL 2738220, at *3-4 (E.D. Pa. June 17, 2014) (finding that a defendant "could not have foreseen" the particular circumstances that led to a data breach); *but see In re* Target Corp. Customer Data Sec. Breach Litigation,—F. Supp. 3d—, MDL No. 14–2522, 2014 WL 6775314, at *3-4 (D. Minn. December 2, 2014) (finding that the cyberattack against Target was foreseeable because Target had allegedly affirmatively disabled a security feature that would have prevented the attack).

[243] *See* RESTATEMENT (SECOND) OF TORTS §448 ("The act of a third person in committing an intentional tort or crime is a superseding cause of harm ... unless the actor at the time of his negligent conduct realized or should have realized the likelihood that such a situation might be created, and that a third person might avail himself of the opportunity to commit such a tort or crime.").

[244] *See* Michael L. Rustad & Thomas H. Koenig, *Extending Learned Hand's Negligence Formula to Information Security Breaches,* 3 ISJLP 237, 251 (2007); *see also* Michael L. Rustad &

Thomas H. Koenig, *The Tort of Negligent Enablement of Cybercrime,* 20 BERKELEY TECH. L.J. 1553, 1553 (2005) ("Any duty to protect computer users from the cybercrimes of third persons must be predicated on a preventable risk.").

[245] *See* John A. Fisher, *Secure My Data or Pay the Price: Consumer Remedy for Negligent Enablement of Data Breach,* 4 WM. & MARY BUS. L. REV. 215, 230 (2013).

[246] *See* Palmer, *supra* note 72, at 323 (arguing that tort law creates an "incentive to not meaningfully participate in information sharing by simply staying in the dark and not expose itself to potential liability.").

[247] *See, e.g.,* PRICEWATERHOUSE COOPERS, *supra* note 13, at 10 (noting that the "annual estimated reported average financial loss attributed to cybersecurity incidents was $2.7 million, a jump of 34% over 2013.").

[248] *See* Jacob W. Schneider, Note, *Preventing Data Breaches: Alternative Approaches to Deter Negligent Handling of Consumer Data,* 15 B.U. J. SCI. & TECH. L. 279, 281-82 (2009) ("When an individual's personal information is stolen, there is no guarantee that it will be used fraudulently. In fact, only 2% of stolen credit card information from data breaches is subject to misuse. Of all identity theft reports, only 1.5 to 4% are the result of stolen credit card information. This probability goes down even further when the volume of personal information is large—since identity thieves can only make use of a small number of accounts.").

[249] *See* Randolph v. ING Life Ins. & Annuity Co., 973 A.2d 702, 708 n.9 (D.C. 2009) (collecting cases where courts "have dismissed similar negligence actions for failure to state a claim, or have entered summary judgment for defendants, in the absence of allegations of present injury to plaintiffs.").

[250] *See* Nat'l Research Council, *supra* note 239, at 50.

[251] *See* Sales, *supra* note 26, at 1535.

[252] *See, e.g., In re* Target Corp. Data Sec. Breach Litigation,—F. Supp. 3d.—, MDL No. 14–2522, 2014 WL 7192478, at * 20 (dismissing several tort claims related to Target's 2013 data breach under the economic loss doctrine); *see also In re* TJX Cos. Retail Sec. Breach Litig., 564 F.3d 489, 498 (1st Cir. 2009) ("AmeriFirst says that it did suffer property damage because it had a property interest in the payment card information, which the security breach rendered worthless. Electronic data can have value and the value can be lost, but the loss here is not a result of physical destruction of property."); Cumis Ins. Soc'y, Inc. v. BJ's Wholesale Club, Inc., 918 N.E. 2d 36, 39, 49-51 (Mass. 2009) ("[T]he plaintiffs suffered only economic harm due to the theft of the credit card account information ... the economic loss doctrine barred recovery on their negligence claims.").

[253] The Bipartisan Policy Center has hypothesized that "domain names and companies who host websites" that may be the subject of cyber-threat information may sue "entities that collect and aggregate cyber-threat information," like ISACs, regarding the "accuracy of their data," potentially chilling cyber-information sharing. *See* Bipartisan Policy Center, *supra* note 30, at 9-10. Presumably such a lawsuit would be based on a defamation claim—that is, an allegation that a defendant negligently published an unprivileged, false, and defamatory statement to a third party. *See* RESTATEMENT (SECOND) OF TORTS §558. The study from the Bipartisan Policy Center does not cite to any lawsuits that have been filed against a cyber-information sharing organization or any other accounts of such an organization being threatened with a lawsuit for the publication of cyber-threat information, making it difficult to assess whether such lawsuits have actually chilled information sharing efforts. *See* Bipartisan Policy Center, *supra* note 30, at 9-10. Nonetheless, Congress, in the Communications Decency Act (CDA), has already provided immunity to defamation

lawsuits directed at services that provide information to multiple users by giving them access to a computer server. *See* 47 U.S.C. §230(c)(1). Courts interpreting the CDA have generally agreed that the Act immunizes online information hosts from liability for defamatory material posted through their services by third parties. *See, e.g.,* Zeran v. Am. Online, Inc., 129 F.3d 327, 330 (4th Cir. 1997); Green v. America Online, 318 F.3d 465, 471 (3d Cir. 2003); Universal Communications Systems, Inc. v. Lycos, Inc., 478 F.3d 413, 422 (1st Cir. 2007); Doe v. MySpace, Inc., 528 F.3d 413, 420 (5th Cir. 2008); Fair Hous. Council v. Roommates.com, LLC, 521 F.3d 1157, 1170-71 (9th Cir. 2008); Klayman v. Zuckerberg, 753 F.3d 1354, 1359 (D.C. Cir. 2014). So long as a cyber-information sharing service is not "creating or developing" cyber-threat information and sharing it with other entities, *see Fair Hous. Council of San Fernando Valley,* 489 F.3d at 925, it appears the CDA likely shields such entities from any defamation lawsuits that could potentially chill broader cyber-information sharing efforts.

[254] *See* Collier v. Steinhafel, No. 14-cv-266, Docket #1, Compl. (D. Minn. January 29, 2014).

[255] Even in the context of securities litigation, in addition to state common law breach of fiduciary duty claims, federal law allows a private actor to sue as a result of a material misstatement or omission in connection with the purchase or sale of any security, *see* Halliburton Co. v. Erica P. John Fund, Inc., 134 S. Ct. 2398, 2407 (2014), which could plausibly include a claim for failing to disclose cybersecurity risks to investors or federal regulators, *see infra* notes 310-314 and accompanying text.

[256] *See* U.C.C. §4A *et seq.*

[257] Choice Escrow & Land Title, LLC v. BancorpSouth Bank, 754 F.3d 611, 616 (8th Cir. 2014).

[258] *Id.*

[259] *Compare id.* at 622 (concluding that a bank's security procedures, which included password protection, daily transfer limits, device authentication, and dual control, were "commercially reasonable") *with* Patco Constr. Co. v. People's United Bank, 684 F.3d 197, 212 (1st Cir. 2012) (concluding that a "one-size-fits-all" security procedure that provided the same security to all wire transfers regardless of size was commercially reasonable).

[260] *Compare Choice Escrow,* 754 F.3d at 620 (holding that where a bank was aware of a new cyber-threat, offered its customer an updated security procedure to combat the new cyber-threat, and the customer declined to utilize the new security procedure, the bank acted in a commercially reasonable way) *with Patco Constr. Co.,* 684 F.3d at 213 (concluding that a bank's failure to implement additional security procedures was "especially unreasonable in light of the bank's knowledge of ongoing fraud.").

[261] *See* Peretti, *supra* note 32, at 6.

[262] *Id.*

[263] *See supra* note 93 and accompanying text.

[264] See Lisa O. Monaco, Remarks as Prepared for Delivery by Assistant to the President for Homeland Security and Counterterrorism Lisa O. Monaco Strengthening our Nation's Cyber Defenses, (February 11, 2015), available at http://www.whitehouse.gov/the-press-office/2015/02/11/remarks-prepared-delivery-assistant-president-homelandsecurity-and-coun.

[265] These legal issues related to compelled disclosures of cyber-intelligence are beyond the scope of this report. For background on the various methods the government could use to compel a private actor to disclose cyber-intelligence, *see* CRS Report 95-1135, *The Federal Grand Jury*, by Charles Doyle; *see also* CRS Report R41733, *Privacy: An Overview of the Electronic Communications Privacy Act*, by Charles Doyle; CRS Report RL33320,

National Security Letters in Foreign Intelligence Investigations: Legal Background, by Charles Doyle.

[266] The Critical Infrastructure Information Act of 2002 defines the term "voluntary"—in the context of cyber information sharing—as the "submittal of critical infrastructure information to a covered Federal agency

[267] *See* 6 U.S.C. §121(d)(1).

[268] *See* 6 U.S.C. §148(c)(1).

[269] *See* 6 U.S.C. §133.

[270] *See* Broggi, *supra* note 31, at 658-59.

[271] For example, if a successful cyberattack obtained trade secret information from a company, and that company wanted to disclose details about the cyberattack to the government, the cyber-information disclosed could include details and descriptions about the "type and value of compromised data." *See* Emily Frye, *The Tragedy of the Cybercommons: Overcoming Fundamental Vulnerabilities to Critical Infrastructures in a Networked World,* 58 BUSLAW 349, 375 (2002).

[272] *See* Bipartisan Policy Center, *supra* note 30, at 6; *see also see* Zheng and Lewis, *supra* note 32, at 5 (Risk of public disclosure of information shared with the government and potential use of the information in regulatory actions ahve a chilling effect on voluntary cyber threat information sharing.").

[273] *See* 5 U.S.C. §552(a).

[274] CII is statutory defined as "information not customarily in the public domain and related to the security of critical infrastructure or protected systems," including information about (1) actual or potential conduct that would be illegal or harm interstate commerce or threaten public health or safety; (2) vulnerabilities that would prevent the ability to resist such conduct; or (3) any strategies to better protect critical infrastructure systems from such conduct. 6 U.S.C. §131(3).

[275] The CIIA uses the phrase "covered Federal agency" as the entity to whom voluntarily shared CII can be submitted in order to receive protections under Section 214. *See* 6 U.S.C. §133(a). Nonetheless, the CIIA defines the phrase "covered Federal agency" to mean DHS. *See id.* §131(2).

[276] *See* 6 U.S.C. §133(a)(1)(A) ("[C]ritical infrastructure information ... that is voluntarily submitted to a covered agency for use by that agency regarding eh security of critical infrastructure and protected systems, analysis, warning, interdependency study, recovery, reconstitution, or other information purpose, when accompanied by an express statement ... shall be exempted from disclosure ... under section 552 of title 5, United States Code.... "). The CIIA also exempts CII from state or local laws requiring the disclosure of information or records. *See id.* §133(a)(1)(E)(i).

[277] *See* 6 C.F.R. part 29.

[278] 6 U.S.C. §133(a)(1)(A).

[279] 6 U.S.C. §101(4) (citing 42 U.S.C. §5195c(e)).

[280] *See* Dep't of Homeland Sec., *What is Critical Infrastructure,* (November 1, 2013), *available at* http://www.dhs.gov/ what-critical-infrastructure; *cf.* Remijas v. Neiman Marcus Group, LLC, No. 14-C-1735, 2014 WL 4627893, at *2 (N.D. Ill. September 16, 2014) (noting that "cyber-attack/credit card cases" do not "implicate ... questions of national security.")

[281] 6 U.S.C. §133(a)(1)(A).

[282] *See supra* note 274.

[283] 6 U.S.C. §131(3).

[284] *See generally* Kenneth Einar Himma, *Legal, Social, and Ethical Issues of the Internet, in* 1 HANDBOOK OF INFORMATION SECURITY 247, 259-60 (Hossein Bidgoli, ed., 2006) (discussing the difficulty with ascribing meaning to the term "security" in the context of computer security).

[285] *See* Peretti, *supra* note 32, at 5.

[286] *See* 6 C.F.R. §29.6(a)(1); *see also id.* §29.6(a)(3)-(4).

[287] *See* Peretti, *supra* note 32, at 6.

[288] For general criticism of the PCII program, *see* Zheng and Lewis, *supra* note 32, at 5-6.

[289] *See* 6 C.F.R. §29.3(a) ("Information that is separately exempt from public disclosure under [FOIA] ... does not lose its separate exemption from public disclosure due to the applicability of these procedures or any failure to follow them.").

[290] 5 U.S.C. §552(b)(4).

[291] *See* Miller, *supra* note 56 (noting that "companies are approaching [DHS's cyber-information sharing] programs cautiously" because of fears about loss of intellectual property rights).

[292] RESTATEMENT (FIRST) OF TORTS §757, cmt. b.

[293] *See* Unif. Trade Secrets Act §1(4).

[294] *See* Unif. Trade Secrets Act §§2-3.

[295] *See* Frye, *supra* note 271, at 375.

[296] *See* Fail-Safe, LLC v. A.O. Smith Corp., 674 F.3d 889, 893 (7th Cir. 2012).

[297] *Id.*

[298] *See* Eric G. Orlinsky, Kathryn L. Hickey, and David T. Shafer, *Cybersecurity: A Legal Perspective,* 47-DEC MDBJ 32, 34 (2014) ("Due in part to the reliance on technology to share information, contractual relationships need to be built, and contractual provisions now need to be crafted, with an eye towards cybersecurity. The method and location of storage, and the means of regulating access to sensitive information are all critical to maintaining cybersecurity when multiple parties are involved in a project. To best protect the intellectual property and information of a business, as well as sensitive customer information, parties should discuss and expressly agree to contractual terms that address the nuances of information-sharing, information management, and security of data.").

[299] *See* Miller, *supra* note 56.

[300] *See* Dep't of Homeland Sec., *Critical Infrastructure and Key Resources Cyber Information Sharing and Collaboration Program,* 1, (no date given) *available at* https://www.us-cert.gov/sites/default/files/c3vp/ CISCP_20140523.pdf.

[301] *See* Jenny Menna, *DHS Information Sharing Update,* contained in *Minutes of Meeting,* INFORMATION SECURITY AND PRIVACY ADVISORY BOARD, (June 12, 2013), *available at* http://csrc.nist.gov/groups/SMA/ispab/documents/minutes/ 2013-06/ispab_ meeting-minutes_june-2013_approved.pdf ("[T] he problem with [the CRADA] is Intellectual Property, and if shared, it would be community property. It is entirely up to the signer to determine if they want their participation / information to be shared."); *see also* Miller, *supra* note 56 ("We talk about legal instruments that enable that sharing and the lawyers at DHS settle on a [CRADA], which among other things stipulates that information shared in a CRADA environment becomes in effect community property so you lose the rights to that intellectual property.") (quoting Gregory Garcia, a former DHS Assistant Secretary for Cybersecurity). For further criticism of the CRADA as a legal instrument used to facilitate cyber-information sharing, *see* Zheng and Lewis, *supra* note 32, at 5 ("The CRADA process is lengthy and resource-intensive, requiring significant involvement of companies' legal counsel.").

[302] *See also* Miller, *supra* note 56 (quoting Gregory Garcia, a former DHS Assistant Secretary for Cybersecurity).

[303] *See* Peretti, *supra* note 32, at 6; *see also* Fairborz Farahmand, et al. *Evaluating Damages Caused by Information Systems Security Incidents,* in ECONOMICS OF INFORMATION SECURITY 96 (eds. L. Jean Camp and Stephen Lewis) (2004) ("[C]ompanies are reluctant to give the government information on attacks and vulnerabilities that regulators may use against them later on.").

[304] *See* Peretti, *supra* note 32, at 6.

[305] *See* 15 U.S.C. §45.

[306] *See To Business' Chagrin, Cybersecurity Is FTC's Turf Now,* LAW 360, (June 10, 2014), *available at* http://www.law360.com/articles/545258/to-business-chagrin-cybersecurity-is-ftc-s-turf-now; *see also* Julie Brill, *On the Front Lines: The FTC's Role in Data Security*, Keynote Address Before the Center for Strategic and International Studies, (September 17, 2014), *available at* http://www.ftc.gov/system/files/documents/public_statements/582841/140917csisspeech.pdf.

[307] *See* Info. Tech Industry Council, *supra* note 216, at 2 (suggesting as a "potential result" of disclosing cyber intelligence to the government, the FTC could "use[] the information submitted ... as evidence in a case against Company A for violating the security provisions of HIPAA.").

[308] *See* Eva M. Wooten and Lei Shen, *The Curious Case of LabMD: New Developments in the "Other" FTC Data-Security Case,* (August 11, 2014), *available at* http://www.mayerbrown.com/The-Curious-Case-of-LabMD-NewDevelopments-In-The-Other-FTC-Data-Security-Case/. For more on the LabMD litigation, *see* CRS Report R43723, *The Federal Trade Commission's Regulation of Data Security Under Its Unfair or Deceptive Acts or Practices (UDAP) Authority*, by Gina Stevens.

[309] 15 U.S.C. §78d.

[310] *See* James M. Bartos, UNITED STATES SECURITIES LAW: A PRACTICAL GUIDE 2-3 (3d. ed.) (2006).

[311] 15 U.S.C. §§77g, 77j.

[312] See *Disclosure Guidance: Topic No. 2: Cybersecurity*, U.S. Sec. & Exch. Comm'n (October 13, 2011), http://www.sec.gov/divisions/corpfin/guidance/cfguidance-topic2.htm.

[313] *Id.*

[314] *See* Bartos, *supra* note 310, at 2-3.

[315] *See* Info. Tech Industry Council, *supra* note 216, at 3.

[316] *Id.* (fearing that "[g]overnment prosecutors, law enforcement agencies, or civil attorneys" could use cyberintelligence "as the absis for establishing a violation of civil or criminal law" against the company that shared the information).

[317] 6 U.S.C. §133(a)(1)(C).

[318] *Id.* §133(a)(1)(D).

[319] *Id.* §133(f).

[320] *See supra* "Freedom of Information Act Disclosures," pp. 33-35.

[321] *See* 6 U.S.C. §133(a)(1)(C)-(D). The phrase "good faith" is a notoriously "elusive" concept, *see generally* Roger Brownsword et al., "Good Faith in Contract," in GOOD FAITH IN CONTRACT: CONCEPT AND CONTEXT 1 (Roger Brownsword ed., 1999), and it may be equally elusive to divine the general purposes of a law and whether those purposes fit with the particular collateral use in question, *see generally* Davis County Solid Waste Mgmt. v. United States EPA, 101 F.3d 1395, 1409 (D.C. Cir. 1996) ("[I]t is often difficult

to determine whether an interpretation of a statute frustrates or advances congressional purposes.").

[322] *See generally* Geoff Dyer and Hannah Kuchler, *Barack Obama's cyber security push spurs privacy fears*, FINANCIAL TIMES, (February 12, 2015), http://www.ft.com/cms/s/0/64842466-b2b2-11e4-a058- 00144feab7de.html#axzz3T8sCV7hl.

[323] *See* Mark D. Young, *National Insecurity: The Impacts of Illegal Disclosures of Classified Information,* 10 ISJLP 367, 402 (2014) ("Snowden's disclosure of classified information has not only chilled the relationship between Silicon Valley and the U.S. government, but also it has damaged the bottom line for American technology firms ... [R]ecent losses for Google, Cisco, and AT&T can be attributed to the alleged role of American technology companies in the Snowden scandal.").

[324] *See* Gyenes, *supra* note 56, at 304; *see also* Young, *supra* note 323, at 402 ("With their bottom lines at risk, it is understandable that American technology companies would distance themselves from the U.S. government.").

[325] *See* David Inserra and Paul Rosenzweig, *Cybersecurity Information Sharing: One Step Toward U.S. Security, Prosperity, and Freedom in Cyberspace,* HERITAGE FOUNDATION, (April 1, 2014), *available at* http://www.heritage.org/research/reports/2014/04/cybersecurity-information-sharing-one-step-toward-us-security-prosperity-and-freedom-incyberspace#_ftnref17 ("[T]he Stored Communication Act seem[s] to prohibit or potentially prohibit the sharing of cybersecurity information."); *see also* Burstein, *supra* note 134, at 189-90.

[326] *See supra* "The Stored Communications Act," at pp. 18-21.

[327] *See* 18 U.S.C. §2702(a)(3) (excluding from the prohibition on the disclosure of non-content information to a governmental entity "the contents of communication covered by paragraph (1) or (2)). There are specific exceptions to the prohibitions contained in 18 U.S.C. §§2702(a)(1)-(2) based on if the disclosure is made to a governmental entity. For example, the contents of communication can be disclosed: (1) to a law enforcement agency if the contents were inadvertently obtained by the service provider and appear to relate to the commission to a crime, *id.* §2702(b)(7); (2) to a governmental entity if the provider in good faith believes that "that an emergency involving danger of death or serious physical injury to any person requires disclosure without delay of communications relating to the emergency," *id.* §2702(b)(8); (3) pursuant to a warrant if procedures outlined in 18 U.S.C. §2703 are followed, *id.* §§2702(b)(2); and (4) as required by certain provisions of the Foreign Intelligence Surveillance Act of 1978, *see id.* §§2702(b)(2), 2511(2)(a).

[328] *See id.* §2702(a)(3); *see also id.* §2510(6) (defining the term "person" to include "any employee or agent of the United States or any State or political subdivision thereof.... ").

[329] Unlike 18 U.S.C. §2702(a)(1), §2702(a)(3) is not limited to disclosures made by an ECS when the underlying communications are held *in storage*, meaning that the prohibition on disclosing non-content information to the government generally applies to all providers of ECS to the public, which is defined broadly as "any service which provides to users ... the ability to send or receive ... electronic communications," *see* 18 U.S.C. §2510(15).

[330] *Id.* §2702(a)(3).

[331] *See In re* United States ex rel. an Order Authorizing Disclosure of Location Info. of a Specified Wireless Tel., 849 F. Supp. 2d 526, 573 (D. Md. 2011) ("The statute offers no definition nor explanation of what constitutes 'records' or 'information pertaining to a subscriber.'").

[332] *See In re* United States for an Order Directing Provider of Elec. Commun. Serv. to Disclose Records to the Gov't, 620 F.3d 304 (3d Cir. 2010) (noting the breadth of the term "record or

other information pertaining to a subscriber or customer"); *see also In re Zynga Privacy Litig.*, 750 F.3d at 1104 ("Although there is no specific statutory definition for "record," the Stored Communications Act provides examples of record information ... includ[ing] among other things, the 'name,' 'address,' and 'subscriber number or identity' of 'a subscriber to or customer of such service,' but not 'the contents of communications.'"); *see also* Telecomms. Regulatory Bd. v. CTIA, 752 F.3d 60, 68 (1st Cir. 2014) ("[T]he SCA clearly prohibits communications providers from disclosing to the government basic subscriber information— including a customer's name, address, and telephone number—without a subpoena.").

333 *See* Dep't of Justice, *Sharing Cyberthreat Information Under 18 U.S.C. §2702(a)(3)*, (May 9, 2014), at pg. 3, *available at* http://www.justice.gov/criminal/cybercrime/docs/guidance-for-ecpa-issue-5-9-2014.pdf (hereinafter "DOJ White Paper").

334 *Id.*

335 A detailed examination of the merits of the DOJ's interpretation of 18 U.S.C. §2702(a)(3) are beyond the scope of this report. Nonetheless, the DOJ White Paper notes several strong arguments for why the SCA should not bar the government from receiving information that does not identify specific customers or subscribers, including the general purposes of the Act to provide privacy protections for information about individuals that are in the hands of third-party service providers. *See id.* at 4-5. On the other hand, the text of the SCA, while using the article "a" in the phrase "record or other information pertaining to a subscriber ... or customer," *see id.* at 4 (arguing that the use of the singular noun implied Congress was concerned with information as it pertained to a specific identifiable customer), uses the phrase "pertaining to," which has generally been interpreted has having a *very* broad meaning and being synonymous with the phrase "relates to." *See, e.g.*, James Madison Project v. CIA, No. 8-cv-1323, 2009 WL 2777961, at *4 (E.D. Va. August 31, 2009) (noting the breadth of the phrase "pertaining to"). Moreover, the fact that Congress has in other privacy laws explicitly exempted information that does not pertain to a particular individual, *see, e.g.*, 47 U.S.C. §222(c)(3); 47 U.S.C. §551(a)(2)(A), indicates that Congress was interested in protecting a broader set of information than just personally identifiable information with the SCA. *See supra* "Other Federal and State Privacy Laws," at pp. 23-26; *see generally In re* Haas, 48 F.3d 1153, 1156 (11th Cir. 1995) ("Where Congress knows how to say something but chooses not to, its silence is controlling.") (citing Bfp v. Resolution Trust Corp., 511 U.S. 531, 554 (1994)).

336 *See* Inserra and Rosenzweig, *supra* note 325.

337 As the DOJ notes in its White Paper, "determining when data does or does not pertain to a subscriber or customer will be a highly fact-specific inquiry," leaving considerable uncertain with respect to the scope of the SCA even if the DOJ's more narrow interpretation of §2702(a)(3) governed. *See* DOJ White Paper, *supra* note 333, at 7. It is also important to note that the Department of Justice does not enforce §2702 of the SCA, as that section is only enforceable through a private right of action. *See* 18 U.S.C. §2707. In other words, DOJ's position as staked out in the White Paper does nothing to prevent a private actor from suing a service provider for violating §2702(a)(3) by disseminating aggregate cyber-information to the government, and the DOJ's White Paper will receive no deference from a court resolving such litigation. *See* Fed. Labor Relations Auth. v. United States Dep't of Treasury, 884 F.2d 1446, 1451 (D.C. Cir. 1989) (holding that *Chevron* deference should not be afforded to an agency who has no special duty to interpret a particular statute).

338 *See* 18 U.S.C. §2702(b)-(c).

[339] *See id.* §2702(b)(2)&(5) (provider exception with respect to the contents of communication); *id.* §2702(b)(3) (consent exception with respect to the contents of communication); *id.* §2702(c)(3) (provider exception with respect to non-content information); *id.* §2702(c)(2) (consent exception with respect to non-content information).

[340] *See supra* notes 166-167 and accompanying text.

[341] *See supra* notes 164-165 and accompanying text.

[342] *See* 18 U.S.C. §2702(b)(8), (c)(4).

[343] *See* United States v. Caraballo, 963 F. Supp. 2d 341, 361 (D. Vt. 2013); *see also* United States v. Tsarnaev,—F. Supp. 3d.—, No. 13-CR-10200, 2014 WL 5308087, at *8-9 n.2 (D. Mass. October 17, 2014) (finding that the exigent circumstnaces exception to the SCA allowed the government to access an "at large" suspect's emails from Yahoo!); *see generally* United States v. Crouch, 666 F. Supp. 1414, 1416 (N.D. Cal. 1987) (holding that ECPA's emergency authorizations should be read narrowly).

[344] *See, e.g.,* National Cybersecurity and Critical Infrastructure Protection Act of 2014, H.R. 3696, 113th Cong. §103 (establishing a framework for sharing information with at least 16 different industry specific ISACs); Cyber Economic Espionage Accountability Act, S. 111, 113th Cong. §3 (requiring the disclosure by the federal government to the public a "list of persons" responsible for cyber-economic espionage); Cybersecurity Public Awareness Act of 2013, S. 1638, 113th Cong. §3 (requiring several reports listing major cyber incidents involving executive agencies); Cyber Information Sharing Tax Credit Act, S. 2717, 113th Cong. §2 (allowing for tax credits for certain expenses incurred for sharing cyber-intelligence).

[345] *See, e.g.,* Cyber Intelligence Sharing and Protection Act, H.R. 3523, 112th Cong, H.R. 624, 113th Cong, H.R. 234, 114th Cong. (hereinafter "CISPA") (all other references to CISPA will be references to H.R. 234 in the 114th Cong.); Cyber Threat Sharing Act of 2015, S. 456, 114th Cong. (herein "CTSA"); Cybersecurity Information Sharing Act of 2014 , S. 2588, 113th Cong. (hereinafter "CISA"). All references to CISA in this report refer to the 2014 version of the bill. As of publication, the Senate was beginning deliberations on a 2015 version of the bill. *See Discussion Draft*— Cybersecurity Information Sharing Act of 2015, S.---, 114th Cong., *available at* http://www.burr.senate.gov/public/_files/CISA%202015%20Discussion%20Draft.pdf.

[346] 6 U.S.C. §§101 *et seq.*

[347] *See id.* §§121, 143.

[348] *See generally supra* "Sharing Cyber-Information in the Possession of the Government" and "Sharing Cyber Information in the Possession of Private Entities."; *see also* Zheng and Lewis, *supra* note 32, at 8 ("Sharing is not directly authorized by law ... which has created uncertainty around the legality of sharing cyber threat information.").

[349] *See* CISPA §2(b)(4)(C).

[350] *See id.* §3 (enacting §1104(b)).

[351] *See* CTSA §2 (enacting §229(c)(1)).

[352] *Id.* §2 (enacting §229(b)(1)).

[353] *See* CISA §3(a)(2) (allowing for the sharing of "cyber threat indicators" from the federal government to the private sector); *id.* §4(c)(1) (allowing an "entity" to share with or receive from the federal government or "any other entity" "cyber threat indicators" and "countermeasures"); *see generally id.* §1(7) (defining the term "cyber threat indicator" to include (1) malicious reconnaissance (e.g., anomalous patterns of communications); (2) methods of defeating a security control or exploitation of a security control or exploitation of a security vulnerability; (3) security vulnerabilities, (4) methods of causing a user to

unwittingly defeat a control; (5) malicious cyber command and control; (6) actual or potential harm caused by an incident (including information exfiltrated from the information system); (7) any other attribute of a cybersecurity threat); *id.* §1(4)(defining "countermeasure" as "an action, device, procedure, technique, or other measure applied to an information system or information that is stored on, processed by, or transiting an information system that prevents or mitigates a known or suspected cybersecurity threat or security vulnerability.").

354 *See* CTSA §2 (enacting §229(b)-(c)). For example, the CTSA maintains most of the CISA's definition for "cyber threat indicator," but excludes from the definition "actual or potential harm caused by an incident," including data associated with such an incident. *See id.* §2 (enacting §229(a)(3)). Moreover, the CTSA narrows the definition of "cyber threat indicator" in that "reasonable efforts must be made to remove information that may be used to identify specific persons reasonably believed to be unrelated to the cyber threat" for such information to be considered a "cyber threat indicator." *See id.* §2 (enacting §229(a)(3)(B)). The CTSA does not allow private or public entities to share countermeasures as defined by the CISA.

355 *See* CISPA §3 (enacting §1104(b)).

356 *See* WHD §103(b); *see also* CTSA §2 (enacting §229(b)(1)).

357 *See* CISPA §3 (enacting §1104(b)(2)(A)).

358 CISPA does prohibit shared information from being used for an "unfair competitive advantage to the detriment" of the entity that provided the information. *Id.* §3 (enacting §1104(b)(2)(B)).

359 *Id.* §3 (enacting §1104(b)(2)(D)).

360 *See id.* §3 (enacting §1104(f)(8)) (defining cybersecurity purpose to mean "the purpose of ensuring the integrity, confidentiality, or availability of, or safeguarding, a system or network," including protecting a system or network from (1) a vulnerability; (2) a threat to its integrity, confidentiality, or availability; (3) an effort to deny access or degrade, disrupt, or destroy; (4) an effort to gain unauthorized access (other than by solely violating a terms of service agreement).

361 *See* CTSA §2 (enacting §229(b)(3)(C)).

362 *See id.* §2 (enacting §229(b)(3)(A)) (mandating that shared cyber-threat indicators can only be used for the "purpose" of protecting an "information system or information that is stored on, processed by, or transiting an information system from cyber threats;" "identifying or mitigating such cyber threats;" or "reporting a crime."). A cyber threat is defined by the CTSA as "any action that may result in ... unauthorized access" (other than solely violating a terms of service agreement) "in order to damage or impair the integrity, confidentiality, or availability of an information system; or ... unauthorized exfiltration, deletion, or manipulation of information that is stored on, processed by, or transiting an information system." *See id.* §2 (enacting §229(a)(2)).

363 *See id.* §2 (enacting §229(b)(3)(B)).

364 *See, e.g.,* CISPA §3 (enacting §1104(b)(2)) (authorizing the sharing of cyber-threat information, but regulating the use and protection of such information).

365 *See supra* notes 66-71 and accompanying text (on federal authority to distribute cyber-information); *see also supra* notes 267-270 and accompanying text (on federal authority to receive cyber-information from the private sector).

366 *See supra* notes 72-76 and accompanying text.

367 *See, e.g.,* SECURE IT, S. 3342, 112th Cong. §103(a)(1).

[368] *See* CTSA §2 (enacting §229(c)(1) (The Secretary shall designate the [NCCIC] to receive and disclose cyber threat indicators to Federal and non-Federal entities in as close to real time as practicable, consistent with, and in accordance with the purposes of, this section.").

[369] *See* CISPA §2(b)(1).

[370] *See id.* §2(b)(3).

[371] *See id.* §2(b)(2).

[372] *See id.* §2(b)(3).

[373] *See* CISA §3(a).

[374] *Id.* §5(a).

[375] *See id.* §5(c)(1).

[376] *See generally* Washington Gas Light Co. v. Byrnes, 137 F.2d 547, 561 (D.C. Cir. 1943) ("When ... a new law is designed to achieve a clear purpose, it must be respected; and inconsistent procedures, previously existing must be disregarded.").

[377] *See generally* Nat'l Ass'n of Home Builders v. Defenders of Wildlife, 551 U.S. 644, 662 (2007) ("'[R]epeals by implication are not favored' and will not be presumed unless the 'intention of the legislature to repeal [is] clear and manifest.'") (internal citations omitted).

[378] *See* CISPA §6(f)(1).

[379] *See supra* notes 82-87 and accompanying text.

[380] *See supra* notes 88-90 and accompanying text.

[381] *See, e.g.,* CISPA §2(b)(4)(A)-(B) (allowing for real time distribution to other federal entities); CTSA §2 (enacting §229(c)(3)) (same); CISA §5(c)(1)(C) (same).

[382] *See, e.g.,* CTSA §2 (enacting §229(c)) ("The Secretary shall designate the Center to receive and disclose cyber threat indicators to Federal and non-Federal entities in as close to real time as practicable, consistent with, and in accordance with the purposes of, this section."); CISA §3(b)(1).

[383] *See* CISA §§2(8), 5(c).

[384] *See, e.g.,* CTSA §2 (enacting §229(c)(2) (authorizing DHS to coordinate federal efforts to "ensure that useful classified ... cyber threat indicators are shared in a timely manner with non-Federal entities."); CISA §3(a)(1) (authorizing the development of procedures that allow for the "timely sharing of classified cyber threat indicators in the possession of the Federal Government with cleared representatives of appropriate entities."); CISPA §3(a) (enacting §1104(a) (authorizing the DNI to establish procedures regarding the sharing and use of classified cyber-intelligence).

[385] *See* CISPA §3(a) (enacting §1104(a)(1)).

[386] *Id.* §3(a) (enacting §1104(a)(3)).

[387] *See supra* notes 382-384.

[388] *See, e.g.,* Paul Rosenzweig, *Comparing the Senate Cybersecurity Liability Provisions,* LAWFARE, (March 18, 2012), *available at* http://www.lawfareblog.com/2012/03 /comparing-the-senate-cybersecurity-liability-provisions/ (hereinafter "Rosenzweig-Lawfare").

[389] *See generally supra* "Sharing Cyber-Information in the Possession of Private Entities."

[390] *Id.*

[391] *See* Brian B. Kelly, *Investing in a Centralized Cybersecurity Infrastructure: Why 'Hacktivism' Can and Should Influence Cybersecurity Reform,* 92 B.U.L. REV. 1663, 1696 (2012).

[392] *See, e.g.,* CISPA §3 (enacting §1104(b)(3)); CTSA §2 (enacting §229(b)); CISA §6.

[393] *See, e.g.,* Rosenzweig-Lawfare, *supra* note 388.

[394] *See* Nojeim Testimony, *supra* note 132, at 5 ("Companies that share information under such a narrow exception will enjoy the liability protections already built into theses statutes. As

other statutes that limit information sharing for cyber security purposes are identified, Congress may consider additional exceptions.").

395 *Id.* (emphasis added).

396 *See* Sales, *supra* note 26, at 1551.

397 *See generally supra* "Sharing Cyber-Information in the Possession of Private Entities."

398 *See* Ponemon Institute—Threat Intelligence, *supra* note 33, at 3.

399 For example, Professors Rustad and Koenig have written extensively on the need for courts to begin to recognize new torts based on the negligent enablement of cybercrime. *See supra* note 244.

400 *See* Ashcroft v. Iqbal, 556 U.S. 662, 679 (2009). For example, rule of reason antitrust cases often require resolution at the summary judgment as opposed to motion to dismiss stage because of the factually intensive nature of such cases. *See* C. Paul Rogers III, *The Incredible Shrinking Antitrust Law and the Antitrust Gap,* 52 U. LOUISVILLE L. REV. 67, 79 (2013).

401 Litigation costs in a "typical" federal lawsuit were recently estimated at nearly $20,000 for defendants, but in cases involving large corporations discovery expenses can balloon to over $700,000. *See The Costs and Burdens of Civil Discovery: Hearing before the Subcommittee on the Constitution of the Committee on the Judiciary,* 112th Cong, 1st Sess 4-5 (2011) (written statement of William H. J. Hubbard, Ass't. Prof. of Law, University of Chicago Law School). Discovery can be particularly expensive in cases involving electronic data, such as those involving cyber-information, as discovery involving electronic data on average costs of "tens or hundreds of thousands of dollars" in even average cases. *See* Scott A. Moss, *Litigation Discovery Cannot be Optimal but Could be Better: The Economics of Improving Discovery Timing in a Digital Age,* 58 DUKE L.J. 889, 894 (2009).

402 *See, e.g.,* CISPA §3 (enacting §1104(b)(1)-(2); CTSA §2 (enacting §229(b)(1)); CISA §4(c)(1).

403 *See* CISA §4(c)(1).

404 *See In re* Robinson, 764 F.3d 554, 560 (6th Cir. 2014); Gonzales v. Arrow Fin. Servs., LLC, 660 F.3d 1055, 1066 n.8 (9th Cir. Cal. 2011); Multi-State Communications, Inc. v. FCC, 728 F.2d 1519, 1525 (D.C. Cir. 1984).

405 *See, e.g.* CISPA §3 (enacting §1104(b)(3)) ("No civil or criminal cause of action shall lie or be maintained in Federal or State court ... for using cybersecurity systems to identify or obtain cyber threat information or for sharing such information in accordance with this section; or ... for decisions made for cybersecurity purposes and based on cyber threat information identified, obtained, or shared under this section."); CTSA §2 (enacting §229(d)(1)(A)) ("A civil or criminal action may not be filed or maintained in a Federal or State court against an entity for the voluntary disclosure or receipt under this section of a lawfully obtained cyber threat indicator, that the entity was not otherwise required to disclose, to or from ... [the NCCIC] or a [self-certified ISAO]."); CISA §6(a)-(b) ("No cause of action shall lie or be maintained in any court against any private entity, and such action shall be promptly dismissed, for the monitoring of information systems and information ... [and] the sharing or receipt of cyber threat indicators or countermeasures.... ").

406 *See* CISPA §3 (enacting §1104(b)(3)(B)) (exempting from the liability limitation clause any acts that lack good faith, including "any act or omission taken with intent to injure, defraud, or otherwise endanger any individual, government entity, private entity, or utility."); CISA §6(c) ("[A] good faith reliance by an entity that the conduct complained of was permitted under this Act shall be a complete defense against any action brought in any court against such entity.").

[407] *See, e.g.*, CISPA §3 (enacting §1104(e) ("This section supersedes any statute of a State or political subdivision of a State that restricts or otherwise expressly regulates an activity authorized under subsection (b)."); CTSA §2 (enacting §229(f)(2)) ("This section supersedes any law or requirement of a State or political subdivision of a State that restricts or otherwise expressly regulates the retention, use, or disclosure of a cyber threat indicator by a private entity."); CISA §8(j)(1) ("This Act supersedes any statute or other law of a State or political subdivision of a State that restricts or otherwise expressly regulates an activity authorized under this Act.").

[408] *See* CTSA §2 (enacting §229(d)(1)(A)).

[409] *See id.* §2 (enacting §229(a)(3)(B)).

[410] *See* CISA §6(a)-(b).

[411] *See id.* §8(e) (allowing claims based "price-fixing, allocating a market between competitors, monopolizing or attempting to monopolize a market, boycotting or exchanges of price or cost information, customer lists, or information regarding future competitive planning).

[412] *See id.* §6(e).

[413] *See, e.g.*, Rosenzweig-Lawfare, *supra* note 388 ("Of course, 'good faith' is a fact bound issue and will generate litigation."); Miccosukee Tribe of Indians of Fla. v. United States Army Corps of Eng'rs, 619 F.3d 1289, 1298 (11th Cir. 2010) (noting the limitations of a "notwithstanding clause").

[414] *See* 6 U.S.C. §143(1).

[415] *See, e.g.*, Gyenes, *supra* note 56, at 295 ("A simpler plan could push 'critical' industry to improve its cybersecurity.... ."); Broggi, *supra* note 31, at 674-75 ("Congress could mandate that the private sector share certain cybersecurity information with the government."); Sales, *supra* note 26, at 1549 ("The government could require firms to gather information about the vulnerabilities in their systems, the type of attacks they have suffered, and the countermeasures they have used to combat malware, and then to disseminate the date to designated recipients.").

[416] *See* U.S. CONST. am. IV.

[417] Burdeau v. McDowell, 256 U.S. 465, 475 (1921).

[418] *See* United States v. Souza, 223 F.3d 1197 (10th Cir. 2009); *see also* United States v. Momoh, 427 F.3d 137, 140-41 (1st Cir. 2005) (using a multi-factor test, as opposed to the *Souza* test, to distinguish private and government action for Fourth Amendment purposes that included the following factors: "the extent of the government's role in instigating or participating in the search, its intent and the degree of control it exercises over the search and the private party, and the extent to which the private party aims primarily to help the government or to serve its own interests."); *see generally* CRS Report WSLG481, *CISPA, Private Actors, and the Fourth Amendment*, by Richard M. Thompson II (discussing the Fourth Amendment and its application to private actors engaging in computer searches).

[419] *See* Broggi, *supra* note 31, at 675 ("[A] mandate would render scanning pursuant to the ECS program a government search within the meaning of the Fourth Amendment.").

[420] *See* Smith v. Maryland, 442 U.S. 735, 742 (1979).

[421] *See* Schneckloth v. Bustamonte, 412 U.S. 218, 219 (1973).

[422] *See* United States v. Angevine, 281 F.3d 1130, 1134-1135 (10th Cir. 2002).

[423] *See* Griffin v. Wisconsin, 483 U.S. 868, 873 (1987).

[424] *See* Illinois v. Lidster, 540 U.S. 419, 426-27 (2004).

[425] *See* Wooley v. Maynard, 430 U.S. 705, 714 (1977).

[426] *See, e.g., id.; see also* W. Va. State Bd. of Educ. v. Barnette, 319 U.S. 624, 642 (1943) ("If there is any fixed star in our constitutional constellation, it is that no official, high or petty,

can prescribe what shall be orthodox in politics, nationalism, religion, or other matters of opinion or force citizens to confess by word or act their faith therein.")

[427] *See* Rumsfeld v. Forum for Academic & Institutional Rights, Inc., 547 U.S. 47, 61 (2006).

[428] *See generally* Riley v. Nat'l Federation of the Blind of North Carolina, Inc., 487 U.S. 781, 797-98 (1988) (holding that a speaker "has the right to tailor the speech, applies not only to expressions of value, opinion, or endorsement, but equally to statements of *fact* the speaker would rather avoid."); *see* James T. O'Reilly, *"Access to Records" Versus "Access to Evil:" Should Disclosure Laws Consider Motives as a Barrier to Records Release?,* 12 KAN. J.L. & PUB. POL'Y 559, 560 & n.6 (2003) (suggesting that compelled disclosure of cyber threat information may implicate First Amendment interests).

[429] *See, e.g.,* Zauderer v. Office of Disciplinary Counsel of the Supreme Court of Ohio, 471 U.S. 626, 650-53 (1985).

[430] *Cf.* Virginia State Bd. of Pharmacy v. Virginia Citizens Consumer Council, 425 U.S. 748, 772 n.24 (1976) (describing commercial speech as speech that "does 'no more than propose a commercial transaction.'") (internal citations omitted).

[431] *See Riley*, 487 U.S. at 797-98.

[432] *See supra* notes 12-35 and accompanying text.

[433] *See generally* Robert Post, *Compelled Subsidization of Speech:* Johanns v. Livestock Marketing Assocation, 2005 Sup. Ct. Rev. 195, 213-14 & n.92-97 ("[T]he First Amendment is not triggered by all government compulsions to speak. In fact we experience such compulsions all the time, and no one regards them as raising constitutional issues. Examples range from compulsory jury service, to compulsory testimony before courts and legislatures, to compulsory reporting of vehicle accidents, to compulsory reporting of potential public health risks like those involving child abuse, to the myriad of public disclosures required by securities regulation, to the labeling requirements routinely required on consumer products.").

[434] *See* Laura J. Hendrickson, *State Government Speech in a Federal System,* 6 CARDOZO PUB. L. POL'Y & ETHICS J. 691, 706 (2008) (noting that "confusing line of cases defines the doctrine on compelled speech.").

[435] For example, one could envision Fifth Amendment interests being implicated if an individual was, under the threat of legal compulsion, forced to reveal facts about a cyberattack that would incriminate them in some criminal activity. *See generally* Doe v. United States, 487 U.S. 201, 212 (1988). Similarly, the Fifth Amendment may be implicated if a law required the disclosure of cyber-intelligence that altered a business's investment-backed expectation of confidentiality in that information, amounting to a taking lacking just compensation. *See* Ruckelshaus v. Monsanto Co., 467 U.S. 986, 1002-04 (1984).

[436] *See* Sales, *supra* note 26, at 1549 ("Imposing such an obligation would not eliminate companies' incentives to withhold cyber-security data. It would simply make it more costly for them to do so, where costs include the sanctions for hoarding discounted by the probability of punishment. Firms will be more likely to collect and share cyber-security data, but some will still find it advantageous to hoard.").

[437] *See* Broggi, *supra* note 31, at 675.

[438] *See* CISPA §3 (enacting §1104(c)(3)).

[439] *See* CTSA §2 (enacting §229(e)(6)).

[440] *See* CISA §8(f)(3).

[441] *See* Bambauer, *supra* note 34, at 1046 (listing various disincentives for information sharing).

[442] *See* Nojeim-Cybersecurity, *supra* note 33, at 128.

[443] *See* Sales, *supra* note 26, at 1550.

[444] *See id.*

[445] *See* Cyber Information Sharing Tax Credit Act, S. 2717, 113th Cong. §2.

[446] *See* Sales, *supra* note 26, at 1550 ("If the subsidies are large enough, firms will have an incentive not just to report the data they have already compiled, but to invest in discovery previously unknown vulnerabilities, threats, and countermeasures.").

[447] *See supra "Sharing Cyber -Information with the Government,"* at pp. 32-41.

[448] *See* CISPA §3 (enacting §1104(b)(2)(D)(i)); CTSA §2 (enacting §229(d)(2)(A)(i)); CISA §5(d)(3).

[449] *See* CISPA §3 (enacting §1104(b)(2)(D)(i)).

[450] *See* CISA §5(d)(3).

[451] CTSA is the only pending cybersecurity legislation that explicitly amends the CIIA. The bill does this by extending §214 of the Homeland Security Act to cover any "cyber threat indicators" that are submitted by a nonfederal entity to the NCCIC and by excepting from the CIIA's procedural requirements respecting a written statement and acknowledgment of receipt any cyber threat indicators shared under the CTSA. *See* CTSA §2 (enacting §229(d)(2)(B)).

[452] *See* CISPA §3 (enacting §1104(b)(2)(D)(ii)); CISA §5(d)(1)-(2); CTSA §2 (enacting §229(e)(1)(B)(iv).

[453] *See* CISPA §3 (enacting §1104(b)(2)(D)(ii)).

[454] *See* CISA §5(d)(1).

[455] *See* CISPA §3 (enacting §1104(b)(2)(D)(iii)); CISA §§5(d)(5)(D), 8(k); CTSA §2 (enacting §229(d)(3)).

[456] *See* CISPA §3 (enacting §1104(c)(1)(A)-(D)); CISA §5(d)(5)(A)(i)-(iv); CTSA §2 (enacting §229(e)(1)(B)(iii)(I)- (IV)). The CTSA does not use the phrase "cybersecurity purposes," but does restrict the use of a cyber threat indicator by a federal entity for the purpose of protecting "information systems from cyber threats. *See* CTSA §2 (enacting §229(e)(1)(B)(ii)).

[457] *See* CISPA §2(b)(5)(A) (requiring the Secretary of DHS, the Attorney General, the Director of National Intelligence, and the Secretary of Defense to "jointly establish and periodically review policies and procedures governing the receipt, retention, use, and disclosure of non-publicly available cyber threat information shared with the Federal Government" in order to (1) "minimize the impact on privacy and civil liberties," (2) "reasonably limit the receipt, retention, use, and disclosure of cyber threat information associated with specific persons" that is unrelated to a cyber-threat; (3) "safeguard non-publicly available cyber threat information that may be used to identify specific persons from unauthorized access or acquisition;" and (4) protect the "confidentiality of cyber threat information associated with specific persons to the greatest extent practicable"); CISA §3(a) (requiring DNI, DHS, DOD, and DOJ, " in consultation with the heads of the appropriate Federal entities," to jointly promulgate procedures regarding sharing of cyber threat indicators that are "consistent with ... the protection of privacy and civil liberties"); *id.* §3(b) (requiring DOJ to "develop and periodically review guidelines relating to privacy and civil liberties which shall govern the receipt, retention, use, and dissemination of cyber threat indicators by a Federal entity obtained in connection with activities authorized in this Act."); CTSA §2 (enacting §229(d)(3)) (requiring the Secretary of DHS, in consultation with the "Attorney General, the Chief Privacy Officer of the Department, the Chief Privacy and Civil Liberties Officer of the Department of Justice, the Secretary of Commerce, the Director of National Intelligence, the Secretary of Defense, the Director of the Office of Management and Budget, the heads of sector-specific agencies and other appropriate agencies, and the

Privacy and Civil Liberties Oversight Board," to "develop and periodically review policies and procedures governing the receipt, retention, use, and disclosure of a cyber threat indicator obtained by a Federal entity.... ").

[458] *See, e.g.*, CISA §5(b)(2) (describing the content of potential privacy regulations, including the need of such rules to include "requirements to safeguard cyber threat indicators containing personal information of or identifying specific persons.").

[459] *See* CISPA §3 (enacting §1104(b)(4) (prohibiting the government from using shared information that includes library circulation records, library patron lists, book sales records, book customer lists, firearms sales records, tax return records, educational records, and medical records).

[460] *See id.* §3 (enacting §1104(b)(2)).

[461] *See* CISA §5(d)(5)(C)(ii).

[462] *See, e.g.*, CISPA §2(c)(1) (requiring the DHS Inspector General to annually submit to Congress a report reviewing "the use of information shared with the Federal Government under" CISPA); CISA §7(a) (requiring the "heads of the appropriate Federal entities" to biennially submit to Congress a detailed report concerning the implementation of CISA); CTSA §2 (enacting §229(c)(2)(B) (requiring an annual report from DHS be submitted to Congress that reviews cyber threat indicator sharing under CTSA).

[463] *See, e.g.*, CISPA §2(c)(2) (requiring DHS's Officer for Civil Rights and Civil Liberties to annually submit to Congress a report "assessing the privacy and civil liberties impact of the activities conducted by the Federal Government" under CISPA); CISA §7(b) (requiring the Privacy and Civil Liberties Oversight Board and the Inspector Generals of several federal agencies to biennially submit to Congress several detailed report assessing the privacy and civil liberties impact of CISA); CTSA §2 (enacting §229(e)(4) (requiring an annual report from the Chief Privacy of Officer and Chief Privacy and Civil Liberties Officer of DHS be submitted to Congress that assesses "the privacy and civil liberties impact of the governmental activities conducted under" the CTSA).

[464] *See* CTSA (enacting §229(e)(1)(B)(v)).

[465] *See* CISPA §3 (enacting §1104(d)).

[466] *See* 6 U.S.C. §133(f). Moreover, generally where a party wishes to challenge an agency action as violating a federal law or regulation, the Administrative Procedure Act remains as a means to test the legality of the underlying federal agency action. *See* Clouser v. Espy, 42 F.3d 1522, 1528 n.5 (9th Cir. 1994) (citing Lujan v. National Wildlife Federation, 497 U.S. 871(1990)).

[467] *See, e.g.*, CTSA (enacting §229(c)(1) (requiring NCCIC to "receive and disclose cyber threat indicators to Federal and non-Federal entities in as close to real time as practicable.").

[468] *But see* Zheng and Lewis, *supra* note 32, at 8 (arguing that "[s]ecurity and privacy are not mutually exclusive.").

[469] *See* Howard A. Schmidt, *White House Cybersecurity Coordinator, Legislation to Address the Growing Danger of Cyber-Threats,* (January 26, 2012), *available at* http://www.whitehouse.gov/blog/2012/01/26/legislation-addressgrowing-danger-cyber-threats ("[O]nly providing incentives for the private sector to share more information will not, in and of itself, adequately address critical infrastructure vulnerabilities.").

In: Cybersecurity and Cyber-Information Sharing ISBN: 978-1-63483-137-6
Editor: Julia M. Morgan

Chapter 2

LEGISLATION TO FACILITATE CYBERSECURITY INFORMATION SHARING: ECONOMIC ANALYSIS*

N. Eric Weiss

SUMMARY

Data breaches, such as those at Target, Home Depot, Neiman Marcus, JPMorgan Chase, and Anthem, have affected financial records of tens of millions of households and seem to occur regularly. Companies typically respond by trying to increase their cybersecurity, hiring consultants, and purchasing new hardware and software. Policy analysts have suggested that sharing information about these breaches could be an effective and inexpensive part of improving cybersecurity. Firms share information directly on an ad hoc basis and through private-sector, nonprofit organizations such as Information Sharing and Analysis Centers (ISACs) that can analyze and disseminate information.

Firms sometimes do not share information because of perceived legal risks, such as violating privacy or antitrust laws, and economic incentives, such as giving information that will benefit their competitors. A firm that has been attacked might prefer to keep such information private out of a worry that its sales or stock price will fall. Further, there

* This is an edited, reformatted and augmented version of a Congressional Research Service publication R43821, prepared for Members and Committees of Congress, dated February 23, 2015.

are no existing mechanisms to reward firms for sharing information. Their competitors can take advantage of the information, but not contribute in turn. This lack of reciprocity, called "free riding" by economists, may discourage firms from sharing. Information that is shared may not be applicable to those receiving it, or it might be difficult to apply.

Because firms are reluctant to share information, other firms suffer from vulnerabilities that could be corrected. Further, by not sharing information about effective cybersecurity products and techniques, the size and quality of the market for cybersecurity products suffer.

Some industry leaders call for mandatory sharing of information concerning attacks. Other experts advocate a strictly voluntary approach, because they believe it could impose fewer regulatory costs on businesses and cost less for taxpayers.

Several bills introduced in the 113th Congress would have encouraged information sharing. H.R. 624, the Cyber Intelligence Sharing and Protection Act (CISPA), and S. 2588, the Cybersecurity Information Sharing Act (CISA) of 2014, sought to increase information sharing by directing the Department of Homeland Security and the Department of Justice to develop procedures for receiving and sharing information and by providing liability protection for private entities acting in good faith for a cybersecurity purpose. H.R. 624 passed the House, and S. 2588 was reported out of the Senate Select Committee on Intelligence.

Supporters of these two bills argued that they would make cyberspace more secure by increasing the amount and impact of information shared without significantly increasing costs to businesses or taxpayers. The bills would have resolved certain legal issues pertaining to sharing information but did not address the question of why a company would find it in their interest to help a competitor. Opponents of the bills argued that they would have made it legal for companies to retaliate against cyberattacks—which could hurt innocent third parties—and raised privacy concerns by allowing firms to share personally identifiable information with government agencies and other companies.

H.R. 624 and S. 2588 might have increased the likelihood of informal information sharing networks developing. Although informal networks might lack the technical capabilities of an ISAC, they could be more flexible and discourage free-riding by cutting "takers" out of the network, which would alter the competitive incentives in favor of more information sharing. A third bill, S. 2727, the Cyber Information Sharing Tax Credit Act, might have increased information sharing by providing a 100% tax credit for the costs of joining ISACs. No hearings were held on S. 2727.

This report analyzes the incentives for companies to share information about cybersecurity breaches with other companies and the federal government.

INTRODUCTION

Cybercrime continues to increase. The media reports data breaches exposing tens of millions of personal financial records at retailers such as Target, Home Depot, and TJ Maxx. The Ponemon Institute, an independent research institute, estimates that in 2013 the number of attacks on 59 companies based in the United States increased over that of 2012 and the average cost per attack also increased.[1] The Ponemon study found the average cost of a cybercrime incident in FY2014 was $12.7 million compared with $11.6 million in FY2013.

The Center for Strategic and International Studies estimates that cybercrime costs the global economy about $445 billion in a typical year.[2] The risks to critical infrastructure and national security from cyberattacks are harder to quantify, but the Bipartisan Policy Center recently concluded that the United States has a "September 10th ability to guard against cyberattacks."[3] President Obama and some Members of Congress have identified increasing cybersecurity as a priority.[4]

It would seem that companies could increase their cybersecurity at relatively little cost by sharing information about cyberattacks. The costs of a data breach can include detection, containment, repair, incident response, investigation, fraud losses, and lost sales. The cost of sharing information, including joining a specialized sharing organization, is likely to be less than $100,000.[5]

One obstacle to reducing cybercrime is misaligned incentives, which reduce information sharing about cyberattacks. In the aftermath of a cyberattack, at least four groups could be notified: law enforcement, other companies, customers, and (for public companies) stockholders. In addition, certain regulated companies, such as banks and electrical utilities, could be required to notify their regulators of cyberattacks.

If companies notify law enforcement—typically either the Federal Bureau of Investigation (FBI) or the Secret Service—they do so in the hope that those responsible will be brought to justice and that some sort of recovery can be made. They notify other companies in the hope that greater information sharing will improve security. Customers are notified so that they can monitor their financial information to prevent financial fraud. The Securities and Exchange Commission (SEC) requires publicly traded companies to announce information that could affect investors' decisions to invest in a company.

This report analyzes information sharing by government with private companies, by private companies with the government, and among private companies. Sharing information with consumers is mentioned but is not the central focus of this report.

A CYBERSECURITY PROBLEM: MISALIGNED INCENTIVES

Understanding the economic incentives involved in cybersecurity and information sharing can improve the analysis of cybersecurity.

Companies that suffer a cybersecurity breach such as the theft of credit card information do not pay the full cost of the breach. Retailers honoring stolen credit cards have charges reversed (so-called chargebacks) and end up without merchandise or payment. Credit card issuers say that they are not fully compensated for replacing stolen cards.[6] Consumers must monitor their financial accounts and update automated bill payment accounts to guard against cyberattacks.[7]

Meanwhile, software companies frequently weigh the benefits of delays to improve security against the costs of late releases.[8] According to some industry observers, software developers can be under pressure to "ship early, ship often" and fix security and other bugs in a later iteration.[9] Similarly, companies may act in ways that they believe will preserve or increase their market share or profitability even at the expense of cybersecurity.

THE PROBLEM OF UNDERUSED INFORMATION

Many in the cybersecurity field have suggested increasing cybersecurity information sharing between individuals, companies, non-governmental organizations, and governments as a way to increase security.

Many kinds of information can be shared to improve cybersecurity. This can include sharing ways to detect specific attacks and more general information about hardware, software, and procedures. It can include specific and general information about recovering from a data breach. The cost of sharing is relatively small, but the benefits can be large. Michael Daniel, the White House cybersecurity coordinator, described information sharing as "critical to effective cybersecurity," and legislation was introduced in 112th and 113th Congresses to promote information sharing.[10]

One kind of information sharing occurs when organizations learn from third parties (such as law enforcement) that information has been compromised.[11] For example, the Secret Service reportedly notified Target[12] and Home Depot[13] that their data systems had been breached.

Information sharing can also flow in the other direction: According to media reports, JPMorgan discovered that it had cybersecurity problems and asked the FBI for assistance.[14]

Sharing information has benefits. If a firm reports a cyberattack, law enforcement can begin searching for those responsible and possibly alert other organizations, which can review their cybersecurity arrangements to prevent similar attacks.

In some cases, broader sharing of information would benefit the attacked firm; if it does not have the resources for defense or other countermeasures, sharing information might allow another entity, such as a security consultant or the software developer, to develop a countermeasure. But sharing cybersecurity information with a competitor can give away security lessons that were learned at great expense. Moreover, some may fear that publicly revealing a cyber breach can scare customers away to competitors leading to reduced revenue and possibly stock price declines. In other words, the hacked company's competitors might benefit from the information or its revenue or stock price might decline.[15]

In 47 states and the District of Columbia, Guam, Puerto Rico, and the Virgin Islands, companies can be required to notify consumers if personally identifiable information (PII) is breached.[16]

Typically, consumers are notified of the breach, advised to monitor financial accounts closely, and sometimes offered free credit monitoring or other assistance.[17] Some, including the chief information officer of the retailer Urban Outfitters, have argued that public disclosure can tip off attackers or waste time if information is breached but not stolen.[18]

Industry participants and outside observers appear to generally agree that there is less than optimal information sharing about attacks.[19] Although the amount of harm caused by inadequate information sharing is hard to measure, and increasing information sharing can be difficult, it has at times increased security. By contrast, while the broad outline of the Target credit card hack[20] had been widely discussed, Home Depot was the victim of a similar attack through a vendor whose security had been compromised.[21]

Information sharing would appear to be a relatively inexpensive way for a group of companies to improve their cybersecurity, but a review of recent data breaches shows that most of the details about breaches are released by third party experts, not the firms involved. The next section analyzes some of the reasons for this apparent reticence by firms.

Perceived Legal Barriers to Information Sharing

Firms and industry groups have expressed reluctance to share information in part because doing so might violate privacy or antitrust laws.[22] Another concern is exposing proprietary business information.[23]

To help assuage these fears, the Department of Justice (DOJ) has provided guidance that it will not consider generally accepted cybersecurity information sharing to be anticompetitive behavior.[24] Some cybersecurity experts, industry participants, and several Members of Congress remain concerned that firms are holding back information that could make cyberspace more secure.[25]

Economic Incentives to Not Share Information

In theory, sharing information about cybersecurity attacks and defenses has many benefits:

- Everyone would appear to benefit from eliminating duplication of costs and efforts.
- Sharing efforts could detect breaches faster and reduce damage caused by breaches.
- Sharing breach information and joint research efforts could lead to new ways to protect information.

In practice, there are also other considerations:

- Some argue that, despite official pronouncements, there are unresolved legal questions concerning privacy and antitrust issues surrounding sharing cybersecurity information.
- Some organizations may be reluctant to help competitors and, in extreme cases, might listen to what others share but offer nothing in return (free-riding in economic terms).
- If the shared information itself is breached by hackers, the organizations could be worse off than if they had not shared the information.
- Public disclosure of a breach may cost an organization customers and sales and affect its stock price.

Although there is some evidence that such fears have been exaggerated, evidence also suggests that they may be the primary factors preventing firms from sharing cybersecurity information.[26]

Comparing Target's stock price to those of three competitors—Walmart, Best Buy, and Costco— from the day before Target's data breach was first revealed on December 18, 2013, to three months afterwards, its stock price increased 19%. In the same time period, Costco's stock price increased 9%, while Walmart's declined 3% and Best Buy's declined 22%.

The Information Sharing and Analysis Center (ISAC) Council emphasized to the Government Accountability Office (GAO) that "the benefits of sharing information are often difficult to discern, while the risks and costs of sharing are direct and foreseeable."[27] A survey of information technology executives found that their chief worry about data breaches was the loss in consumer confidence and resultant decline in revenue, not the losses directly caused by the breach.[28]

Analysis of Firms' Incentives to Share

To understand why companies may not share cybersecurity information, some theoretical scenarios applying basic game theory are examined.

New Threats

Consider a firm that recognizes a new threat or a new (to it, at least) instance of a known threat, one to which its competitors are also potentially vulnerable. There are several possible outcomes depending on the characteristics of the threat and the firms.

If the threat to its profits is small, the firm may or may not choose to develop a countermeasure or share information about the threat, depending on its evaluation of potential reputational benefits for altruistically sharing the information. Some cyberattacks can be viewed as a cost of doing business, much like shoplifting is.

If the threat is significant, the firm may try to develop a custom countermeasure (for instance, hiring a security consultant to create a defense involving new procedures, software, or hardware). If the firm is unable to obtain a countermeasure, it may or may not have financial incentives to share information about the threat, depending on the possibility of another organization developing a countermeasure. Even if the firm believes that developing a countermeasure is unlikely or impossible, there might not be sufficient incentives to share the information compared with the advantages of not sharing with competitors.

Industries making similar products and using similar technologies can benefit more from information sharing, but as they are also more likely to be competitive, they may be less likely to share information.[29] Stronger industry associations could arguably counteract this effect.

Developing and Sharing Countermeasures

If the threat is more general, a firm that develops a countermeasure must decide whether it is better off with the competitive advantage that it now has against selling or giving away the countermeasure. Some firms, such as many in the defense industrial base, also sell cybersecurity services and could decide to sell it, while others, such as those in water treatment, might not be in a position to.

So Why Do Some Firms Share Information?

In most of the scenarios above, organizations might decide not to share information lest they diminish their competitive advantage. So why do organizations sometimes choose to share information?

One reason, as discussed above, may be that the threat is small and the firm wants to cultivate a reputation as a good corporate citizen. The legal requirement to maximize shareholder value does not translate into employing any means necessary to increase the stock price. Cybersecurity is arguably integral to national security and economic growth, and people may choose to share information even when it goes against the balance of their near-term economic incentive to foster a more secure nation and a more productive economy.

Role of Consultants and Insurance Companies in Information Sharing

When an organization calls in outside experts to help after a data breach, these consultants use their accumulated knowledge to investigate, document, and remediate the breach. The contract terms are negotiated between the two parties and generally not disclosed to the public. Following general practices, it is likely that the outside experts agree not to disclose proprietary information. Nevertheless, the consultants leave with knowledge about the data breach, and this information can be used in consulting with other companies.

Following existing practices for property and casualty insurance, companies writing cyberinsurance are likely to assess the cybersecurity practices of a (potential) client. Following a data breach claim, a cyberinsurance company would be likely to conduct or monitor a third-party investigation of the breach. Thus, cyberinsurance companies could gather detailed, technical information on breaches and use this knowledge to prevent future breaches at other clients.

How Can Organizations Share Information?

This section analyzes how organizations share information and legislation that was introduced in the 113th Congress to encourage information sharing.

Categories of Information

Organizations primarily share information about new types of threats, new instances of known threats, and best practices. Information about the effects of an attack can also be shared, even if the method of attack is unknown—for example, by notifying other firms that information has been stolen or that a resource is not operational.

Methods of Information Sharing

Certain types of information can be shared automatically to maximize its value. For instance, when some antivirus software detects malware, it automatically notifies the software vendor, which can analyze the information and update the antivirus software.

Prior to Target's 2013 data breach, which led to the theft of more than 40 million payment card details, Target had recently installed a security system to isolate new malware before it could damage the real system. This software reportedly includes the option to delete malware automatically, but according to a media investigation, "Target's security team turned that function off."[30] The report quoted a chief information security officer of another company who described the choice as normal, because "typically, as a security team, you want to have that last decision point of 'what do I do.'"

Machine autonomy has its issues. Machines generally are not as skilled as individuals in identifying proprietary or PII that should not be shared. Attackers could subvert autonomous information sharing software to further spread their reach or put their attacks on a list of approved programs (a "whitelist"). For effective machine-to-machine sharing to occur, firms need to have high levels of trust with each other and share technical expertise.

Public and Private Sector Information Sharing

Information can be shared within the private sector, within the public sector, and between the two. Government contractors may be subject to more stringent information sharing and disclosure requirements depending on the nature of the work and what department they are working with: the Department of Defense (DOD), for example, requires contractors to report potential exfiltration of classified information.[31] A subset of the private sector, the critical infrastructure industries, operates slightly differently than the rest by relying heavily on Information Sharing and Analysis Centers (ISACs).

ISACs

In 1998, Presidential Decision Directive 63, on critical infrastructure protection, authorized the creation of ISACs and critical infrastructure sector coordinators to assist in their creation.[32]

ISACs are private-sector, nonprofit entities that collect, analyze, and share information on cybersecurity threats and best practices.[33] Some, such as the Defense Industrial Base ISAC and the Oil and Natural Gas ISAC, have mechanisms to share information anonymously between members and with the government. The government also uses ISACs as a tool to communicate with sectors rapidly, particularly in emergency situations. The government also runs some ISAClike entities, such as the Financial Sector Cyber Intelligence Group.[34]

Sectors outside of critical infrastructure have also created ISACs, such as the Retail ISAC. Additionally, the Food ISAC, though classified as a critical infrastructure sector by the DHS, ceased operating due to a lack of information sharing.[35]

The Multi-State ISAC includes all 50 states, four U.S. territories, the District of Columbia, and many local governments. The electricity sector ISAC, run by the North American Electric Reliability Corporation, counts virtually all registered electricity providers as members.

Although the ISACs are sector specific, the multifaceted nature of modern corporations means that these boundaries are not always clear. For example, because the retailer Target owns a bank, the company became the first retailer to join the Financial Services ISAC (FS-ISAC).[36]

Membership in ISACs is voluntary, and levels of participation in ISACs vary. As shown in *Figure 1* and *Figure 2*, the FS-ISAC offers membership tiers ranging from free (with limited benefits) to platinum (with full benefits) and costing $49,950 annually.

This has not equalized the participation rates among firms with varying levels of resources. New York State found that 60% of large banking organizations and 25% of small organizations were members of the FS-ISAC.[37] Nonetheless, the FS-ISAC has helped its members combat cybersecurity issues such as denial-of-service attacks.[38]

Although cybersecurity is important to the information technology industry, the IT-ISAC has 33 members. Many large cybersecurity vendors—such as Symantec, FireEye, and DocuSign—are members but many of the biggest companies in IT, including Google, Mozilla, Adobe, Apple, and Facebook, are not.[39] However, IT-ISAC shares information with other organizations, such as the IT Sector Coordinating Council, which has a broader membership to include, through other alliances, companies such as Google and Facebook.[40]

Generally, ISACs cannot prevent free-riding. If a company joins, there is usually no mechanism preventing it from receiving information even if it does not contribute information of its own. Free-riding has the potential to discourage information sharing. If a sharer consistently contributes without receiving information in return, it may decide that it is helping its competitors more than it is benefitting from sharing.

Mandatory, Voluntary, and Incentivized Sharing

The SEC requires publicly traded companies to disclose "material information," including with regard to cybersecurity risks and cyber incidents. The Supreme Court has ruled that information is material if there is "a substantial likelihood that the disclosure of the omitted fact would have been viewed by the reasonable investor as having significantly altered the 'total mix' of information made available."[41] One open issue is how quickly information must be announced. Cybersecurity breaches can require weeks or months of investigation and remediation.

Compare FS-ISAC Membership Benefits	CNOP Free Join Now	Basic $250.00/yr Join Now
Limited Critical Notifications	✓	✓
CINS Crisis Notifications		✓
24x7 Access to Watch Desk		✓
Cyber/Physical Alerts from Govt, Partners, other ISACs		✓
Cyber/Physical Alerts from Members		✓
Anonymous Submissions		✓
Portal Access Credentials		✓
Document Repository		✓
Member Contact Directory		✓
Risk Mitigation Toolkit		✓
Threat Viewpoints		✓
Daily Report		✓
Monthly Cyber Security Tip Newsletter		✓
Participate in Community Institution Council Teleconferences		✓
Participate in Payment Risk Council Teleconferences		✓
Conduct Member Surveys		✓
Complimentary Webinars		✓
Invitation to Semi-Annual Meetings		✓
Complimentary Regional Workshops		✓
Inclusion in Threat Exercises		✓
Meets Regulatory Compliance Requirement		✓

Source: Financial Services ISAC, Membership Benefits, https://www.fsisac.com/ join.

Figure 1. Financial Services ISAC Membership Tiers.

[illegible]	[illegible]	[illegible]	[illegible]	[illegible]	[illegible]
[illegible]	[illegible]	[illegible]	[illegible]	[illegible]	[illegible]
[illegible]	[illegible]	[illegible]	[illegible]	[illegible]	[illegible]

[illegible]

[illegible]	[illegible]	[illegible]	[illegible]	[illegible]	[illegible]
[illegible]	[illegible]	[illegible]	[illegible]	[illegible]	[illegible]
[illegible]	✓	✓	✓	✓	✓
[illegible]	✓	✓	✓	✓	✓
[illegible]	✓	✓	✓	✓	✓
[illegible]	✓	✓	✓	✓	✓
[illegible]	✓	✓	✓	✓	✓
[illegible]	✓	✓	✓	✓	✓
[illegible]	✓	✓	✓	✓	✓
[illegible]	✓	✓	✓	✓	✓
[illegible]		✓	✓	✓	✓
[illegible]		✓	✓	✓	✓
[illegible]			✓	✓	✓
[illegible]			✓	✓	✓
[illegible]			✓	✓	✓
[illegible]				✓	✓

Source: Financial Services ISAC, Membership Benefits, https://www.fsisac.com/ join.

Figure 2.Financial Services ISAC Membership Tiers.

Law enforcement may be concerned that a public announcement will alert those responsible and allow them to take countermeasures.

As discussed above, DOD is reported to require that its contractors share information on potential security breaches.[42]

Some, such as Dan Geer, chief information security officer of In-Q-Tel (a nonprofit venture capital firm that serves the U.S. intelligence community) have called for mandatory sharing of some information. He has noted that multiple sources have estimated that third parties discover 75% of data breaches. Geer bases his proposed model on the systems used by the aviation industry, which voluntarily reports incidents that had a significant chance of causing damage, and the Center for Disease Control, which mandates reporting incidents above a certain threshold of harm.[43] Other experts advocate a strictly voluntary approach, because they believe it could impose fewer regulatory costs on businesses and cost less for taxpayers.[44]

CONSEQUENCES OF INADEQUATE INFORMATION SHARING

Direct Effects on Security

Inadequate cybersecurity information sharing is thought to result in suboptimal security. By not sharing, organizations might duplicate the same work. If the information is shared—with or without cost—the savings could, in theory, be applied to increasing cybersecurity or some other purpose.

Indirect Security Effects through the Market for Cybersecurity Products

Information differences between buyers and sellers of cybersecurity products could lower the size and quality of the market for cybersecurity products. Cybersecurity can be thought of as an example of a "market for lemons," a concept developed by George Akerlof, which he applied to the used car market.[45]

In a "lemon market," buyers cannot accurately assess a product's value before purchasing it, and sellers cannot credibly disclose the product's value because they have incentives to overstate the quality of their products. If the buyer cannot determine whether the product is better or worse than average, the buyer will be unwilling to pay more than the average price of all the products in the market. This means sellers of better than average quality products have difficulty selling their products for what they are worth, so they underinvest in product development, driving down the overall quality and size of the market.

Security products in general are prone to this problem. It is difficult or impossible to know whether a security product is working because it is good or because the attacks have been weak or few in number. The overall effect is that there are fewer products and relatively fewer good products to choose from, and buyers cannot be confident that they are getting a good value. One result could be less cybersecurity investment than would be optimal.

EFFECTS OF GREATER INFORMATION SHARING

Sharing more information could reduce the information asymmetries and increase the size and quality of the market for cybersecurity products and make cyberspace more secure, allowing firms to better estimate the probability and costs of data breaches, for example. Sharing more information could also reduce duplication of effort, making dollars spent on cybersecurity more effective. Clear metrics of effectiveness and objective, trusted, third-party evaluation services do not appear to currently exist in the cybersecurity market.[46]

The advantages of information sharing are likely to be greatest when organizations are using similar technologies. For example, learning about a weakness in an operating system or application software has the most value to an organization using that operating system or application. It might provide a lesson to those using other software, but it is less likely to be directly applicable.

Another concern is that erroneous information could lead to new security holes. The reputation of those providing information can provide assurance that experts have reviewed and passed on the information.

Currently, a main enforcement mechanism for cybersecurity is the Federal Trade Commission's (FTC's) authority to sue companies for deceptive practices—for example, claiming that their products are "secure" when they do not employ common security practices.[47] Thus, a de facto standard exists for what constitutes acceptable cybersecurity, but it is based on a series of actions taken by organizations that do not need to publicize their security practices. Greater information sharing could make it easier for companies to implement uniform security practices.

Greater information sharing may, in some instances, effectively weaken cybersecurity by creating an overwhelming amount of information, eliminating the capacity to pay attention to truly important alerts. ISACs can help to mitigate this problem by analyzing information and sorting out what information is relevant to subsets of their members.

Some have argued that greater information sharing could encourage the growth of the $1.3 billion cyberinsurance market by allowing for more accurate assessment of risk and security products' effectiveness.[48] A more mature cyberinsurance market would itself make cyberspace more secure: Insurers promote practices that make the insured safer, which would decrease insurers' payouts. Insurers verify and inspect the systems they are insuring. However, some analysts believe that cyberinsurance will have limited utility as many of the losses, such as damage to one's reputation, are intangible and difficult to put a value on.[49]

SELECTED LEGISLATION IN THE 113TH CONGRESS TO ENCOURAGE INFORMATION SHARING

This section provides brief summaries of three bills that were introduced in the 113th Congress.

H.R. 624: The Cyber Intelligence Sharing and Protection Act

The House passed H.R. 624, the Cyber Intelligence Sharing and Protection Act (CISPA), on April 18, 2013.[50] CISPA would have directed the President to designate entities within DHS and DOJ to receive cybersecurity and cybercrime information, respectively, and to develop procedures to ensure real-time sharing with appropriate agencies, cybersecurity providers, and self-protected entities. The bill also would have required the Director of National Intelligence to establish procedures for information sharing with entities and persons with appropriate security clearances.

CISPA would have authorized the government to use shared information for cybersecurity purposes but not for regulatory purposes, and it would have prohibited the use of certain personally identifiable information (PII). CISPA would have exempted information shared with the federal government from public disclosure. The bill specified that it should not be construed to preclude the federal government from requiring an entity to report significant cyber incidents under another provision of law.

CISPA would have authorized cybersecurity providers and self-protected entities to perform cybersecurity activities and share information for a cybersecurity purpose. The bill would have prohibited private entities from using such information to gain a competitive advantage, would have required that they anonymize information to the greatest extent possible, and would have prohibited private entities from using such information for any non-cybersecurity purpose. CISPA also would have provided liability protection from civil or criminal causes of action against private entities acting in good faith for a cybersecurity purpose.

Analysis

CISPA could have increased information sharing. Firms that want to share information but have been advised that it is legally risky would have been more likely to share information. (Although the bill did not address antitrust issues except to say that shared information cannot be used to gain a competitive advantage, the DOJ guidance discussed above addresses this issue.)[51] In particular, CISPA would have aided sharing by firms that were not members of ISACs—smaller firms and firms not in critical infrastructure sectors—because ISACs already perform many of the functions that the government would have performed under CISPA, such as anonymization, sharing, and analysis.

CISPA would not have altered the fundamental economic incentives that cause many companies to choose not to share information, but it had the potential to indirectly allow incentives to change. Firms that perceive information sharing as a potentially profit-diminishing action could still be reluctant to share information. However, by giving companies greater legal protection to share outside of ISACs, informal sharing networks could develop in which companies could exclude free-riders. This would create positive norms of reciprocal sharing and receiving. However, the bill does not guarantee this outcome.

Civil liberties and privacy advocates raised concerns with the bill. Their concerns centered on the fact that H.R. 624 did not specify privacy protections but would have directed DHS, DOJ, the director of National Intelligence, and DOD to promulgate and review procedures to protect privacy and civil liberties rather than specifying those protections in the bill itself.[52]

The Office of Management and Budget (OMB) issued a statement of administration policy expressing President Obama's intent to veto the bill largely due to these privacy concerns.[53]

S. 2588: The Cybersecurity Information Sharing Act

S. 2588, the Cybersecurity Information Sharing Act (CISA), was introduced by Senator Dianne Feinstein and passed by the Senate Select Committee on Intelligence on July 10, 2014. CISA was, in many ways, similar to the House's CISPA. In the 112th Congress, legislation similar to CISA and CISPA was introduced. CISA would have directed the federal government to promulgate information sharing and receiving procedures and policies to protect privacy and civil liberties. CISA also would have limited the federal government's authority to use the information to cybersecurity and cybercrime purposes.

CISA would have provided liability protection for private entities fulfilling cybersecurity purposes in good faith. Additionally, CISA specifically would have exempted good faith sharing of cybersecurity information for cybersecurity purposes from antitrust causes of action—with exceptions to the exemption for certain explicitly anticompetitive behavior.

Unlike CISPA, CISA would have prohibited requiring an entity to provide information to the federal government.

Analysis

Like CISPA, CISA itself would not have fundamentally changed the financial incentives for companies to share information. However, by explicitly providing antitrust protection, the bill would have likely had a greater chance than CISPA of encouraging the development of informal networks with norms of reciprocal sharing. Yet by prohibiting the federal government from requiring the sharing of information, S. 2588 would have deprived the government of a powerful tool that might increase the sharing of cybersecurity information among private-sector participants.

S. 2717: The Cyber Information Sharing Tax Credit Act

S. 2717, the Cyber Information Sharing Tax Credit Act (CISTCA) was introduced in the Senate on July 31, 2013, by Senator Kirsten Gillibrand. The bill would have provided refundable tax credits for all expenses, except travel costs, associated with joining an ISAC.[54]

Analysis

S. 2717 was unusual in providing a 100% tax credit for the action it promotes. More common is for a credit to cover only some of the cost of the action.[55] Under the bill, it would have been in more companies' best interests to join their respective ISACs, because they would have been refunded nearly all of their expenses for joining and participating in their ISACs. [56] Under S. 2717, there would have been little after-tax cost to joining an ISAC.

For many ISACs, the bill would have had little or no impact, as their membership is already at or near 100% of their sectors. However, for other ISACs, such as the retail or IT ISACs, the bill might have increased membership. The costs associated with joining an ISAC can be daunting for smaller firms, as evidenced by their lower rates of participation in the FS-ISAC.[57]

The competitive incentives to not share information would have remained intact. Still, the bill could have increased the amount and spread of information shared.

Other Legislation

In the 112th Congress, S. 3414, the Cybersecurity Act of 2012, would have required critical infrastructure entities to share "significant cyber incidents." S. 3414 would also have provided tangible incentives to share, such as prioritized technical assistance, threat alerts, public recognition, expedited security clearances, and liability protection.[58]

Conclusion: How Might Incentives Change?

Each of these three bills introduced in the 113th Congress aimed to make cyberspace more secure by increasing the amount and impact of information shared while not significantly increasing costs to businesses or taxpayers. They did not address the competitive incentives to not share information.

However, CISPA and CISA would have increased the likelihood of informal information sharing networks developing. Although informal networks might lack the technical capabilities of an ISAC, they can arguably discourage free-riding by cutting "takers" out of the network, which would alter incentives in favor of more information sharing. This arguably requires a serious commitment to prioritizing the good of the sector over the good of the individual firm during the initial phase of informal sharing. CISPA and CISA also could have the likelihood that the markets for cybersecurity products and cyberinsurance will grow in size and quality.

There are other ways that behavior could change: more mandatory information sharing, for example. In 47 states and the District of Columbia, Guam, Puerto Rico, and the Virgin Islands, companies must disclose when PII has been breached. Several bills were introduced that would harmonize this "quilt" of state laws with a federal law.[59] General Motors' recent failure to announce safety information either to the public or senior management arguably warns that disclosure requirements are not always followed.

End Notes

[1] Ponemon Institute, 2014 Cost of Cyber Crime Study: United States, October 2014, https://ssl.www8.hp.com/ww/en/ secure/pdf/4aa5-5208enw.pdf. The Ponemon report looks at the average cost of cybercrime per incident for 59 companies, not the total cost in the United States.

[2] McAfee and the Center for Strategic and International Studies, Net Losses: Estimating the Global Cost of Cybercrime, June 2014, http://www.mcafee.com/us/resources/reports/rp-economic-impact-cybercrime2.pdf.

[3] Bipartisan Policy Center, Reflections on the Tenth Anniversary of the 9/11 Commission Report, Washington, DC, July 2014, p. 7, http://bipartisanpolicy.org/sites/ default/ files/files/%20BPC%209-11%20Commission.pdf. The reference to September 10th is a comparison to the relative lack of airplane security that existed prior to the September 11, 2001 attacks on the World Trade Centers and the Pentagon.

[4] See, for example, U.S. Senate Committee on Homeland Security and Governmental Affairs, "Senator Carper Introduces Bill to Increase Sharing of Cyber Threat Data," press release, February 11, 2015, http://www.hsgac.senate.gov/media/minority-media/senator-carper-introduces-bill-to-increase-sharing-of-cyber-threatdata.

[5] Financial Services ISAC, Membership Benefits, https://www.fsisac.com/join.

[6] Nicholas Ballasy, "Home Depot Breach Costs CUs $60 M," Credit Union Times, October 30, 2014, http://www.cutimes.com/2014/10/30/home-depot-breach-costs-cus-60m.

[7] Tyler Moore and Ross Anderson, Economics and Internet Security: a Survey of Recent Analytical, Empirical, and Behavioral Research, Computer Science Group, Harvard University, 2011, p. 1, ftp://ftp.deas.harvard.edu/techreports/tr-03-11.pdf.

[8] Ross Anderson, "Why Information Security Is Hard—An Economic Perspective," 17th Annual Computer Security Applications Conference, December 10, 2001, http://www.cl.cam.ac.uk/~rja14/Papers/econ.pdf.

[9] Andrew Leonard, "Triumph of the Free-Software Will," Salon, October 31, 2000, http://www.salon.com/2000/10/31/ software_passion/.

[10] For details, see CRS Report R42114, Federal Laws Relating to Cybersecurity: Overview of Major Issues, Current Laws, and Proposed Legislation, by Eric A. Fischer.

[11] Ellen Nakashima, "U.S. Notified 3,000 Companies in 2013 about Cyberattacks," Washington Post, March 24, 2014, http://www.washingtonpost.com/world/national-security/2014/03/24/74aff686-aed9-11e3-96dcd6ea14c099f9_story.html.

[12] Matt Townsend, Lindsey Rupp, and Lauren Coleman-Lochner, "U.S. Secret Service Probes Card Security Breach at Target," Bloomberg, December 19, 2013, http://www.bloomberg.com/news/2013-12-19/u-s-secret-serviceinvestigating-card-security-breach-at-target.html.

[13] Mark Hosenball and Nandita Bose, "UPDATE 3: Home Depot in Contact with Secret Service over Alleged Breach— Source," September 4, 2014, http://www.reuters.com/article/2014/09/04/usa-homedepot-dataprotectionidUSL1N0R517720140904.

[14] Michael Corkery, Jessica Silver-Greenberg, and David E. Sanger, "Obama Had Security Fears on JPMorgan Data Breach," New York Times, October 8, 2014, http://dealbook.nytimes.com/2014/10/08/cyberattack-on-jpmorgan-raisesalarms-at-white-house-and-on-wall-street/.

[15] Academic research suggests that cybersecurity breaches depress stock prices. See, for example, Griselda Sinanaj and Jan Muntermann, "Assessing Corporate Reputational Damage of Data Breaches: An Empirical Analysis," 26th Bled e Conference, Bled, Slovenia, June 2013, https://domino.fov.uni-mb.si/proceedings.nsf/Proceedings/820BFAD242085887C1257B8A002F0B02/$File/07_Sinanaj.pdf; and Edward A. Morse, Vasant Raval, and John R. Wingender Jr., "Market Price Effects of Data Security Breaches," Information Security Journal: A Global Perspective, vol. 20, no. 6 (November 11, 2011), pp. 263-273. For a contrary view by reporters, see Sarah Halzack, "Home Depot and JPMorgan Are Doing Fine. Is It a Sign We're Numb to Data Breaches?" Washington Post, October 6, 2012, http://www.washingtonpost.com/news/get-there/wp/2014/10/06/home-depot-and-jpmorgan-are-doing-fine-is-it-a-signwere-numb-to-data-breaches/.

[16] The definition of PII and the thresholds for consumer notification vary by state. For more information on state laws, see CRS Report R42475, Data Security Breach Notification Laws, by Gina Stevens. PII is any information about an individual maintained by an agency, including (1) any information that can be used to distinguish or trace an individual's identity, such as name, Social Security number, date and place of birth, mother's maiden name, or biometric records; and (2) any other information that is linked or linkable to an individual, such as medical, educational, financial, and employment information. For more on PII, see Erika McCallister, Tim Grance, and Karen Scarfone, "Guide to Protecting the Confidentiality of Personally Identifiable Information (PII): Recommendations of the National Institute of Standards and Technology," U.S. Department of Commerce, National Institute of Standards and Technology, April 2010, p. 2-1, http://csrc.nist.gov/publications/nistpubs/800-122/sp800-122.pdf. See, also, National Council of State Legislatures, "Security Breach Notification Laws," September 3, 2014, http:// http://www.ncsl.org/research/telecommunications-and-information-technology/security-breach-notification-laws.aspx.

[17] For example, see Home Depot's recent data breach announcement. Home Depot, "The Home Depot Completes Malware Elimination and Enhanced Encryption of Payment Data in All U.S. Stores: Provides Further Investigation Details, Updates Outlook," press release, September 18, 2014, https://corporate.homedepot.com/MediaCenter/ Documents/Press%20Release.pdf.

[18] Danny Yadron, "Executives Rethink Merits of Going Public with Data Breaches," Wall Street Journal, August 4, 2013, http://online.wsj.com/articles/a-contrarian-view-on-data-breaches-1407194237?mod=mktw.

[19] Ray Suarez, "Examining Cyber Security with Homeland Security Secretary Janet Napolitano," PBS NewsHour, February 15, 2013, http://www.pbs.org/newshour/bb/science-jan-june13-cybersecurity_02-15/.

[20] For more information about the Target data breach, see CRS Report R43496, The Target and Other Financial Data Breaches: Frequently Asked Questions, by N. Eric Weiss and Rena S. Miller.

[21] Jeffrey Roman, "Home Depot, Target: Same Breach Script," Bank Info Security, November 10, 2014, http://www.bankinfosecurity.com/home-depot-target-same-breach-script-a-7544/op-1.

[22] Securities Industry and Financial Markets Association, "Principles for Effective Cybersecurity Regulatory Guidance," press release, October 20, 2014, http://www.sifma.org/ issues/item.aspx?id=8589951691.

[23] For more information, see CRS Legal Sidebar WSLG483, Obstacles to Private Sector Cyber Threat Information Sharing, by Edward C. Liu.

[24] Department of Justice, "Department of Justice, Federal Trade Commission Issue Antitrust Policy Statement on Sharing Cybersecurity Information," press release, April 10, 2014, http://www.justice.gov/opa/pr/justice-department federal-trade-commission-issue-antitrust-policy-statement-sharing.

[25] Office of Management and Budget, "Statement of Administration Policy, H.R. 624—Cyber Intelligence Sharing and Protection Act," April 16, 2013, http://www.whitehouse.gov /sites/default/files/omb/legislative/sap/113/ saphr624r_20130416.pdf.

[26] See Alessandro Acquisti, Allan Friedman, and Rahul Telang, "Is There a Cost to Privacy Breaches? An Event Study," presented at the Workshop on the Economics of Information Security 2006, http://www.heinz.cmu.edu/ ~acquisti/papers/acquisti-friedman-telang-privacy-breaches.pdf; and Ali Alper Yayla and Qing Hu, "The Impact of Information Security Events on the Stock Value of Firms: The Effect of Contingency Factors," Journal of Information Technology, vol. 26, no. 1 (May 4, 2010), http://www.palgrave-journals.com/jit/journal/v26/n1/abs/jit20104a.html.

[27] U.S. Government Accountability Office, "Critical Infrastructure Protection: Improving Information Sharing with Infrastructure Sectors," July 2004, pp. 9-10, http://www.gao.gov/products/GAO-04-780.

[28] Esther Gal-Or and Anindya Ghose, "The Economic Incentives for Sharing Security Information," Information Systems Research, vol. 16, no. 2 (June 2005), p. 187, http://pages.stern.nyu.edu/~aghose/ISR.pdf.

[29] For more on the effects of product similarity, see Esther Gal-Or and Anindya Ghose, "The Economic Incentives for Sharing Security Information," Information Systems Research, vol. 16, no. 2 (June 2005), p. 187, http://pages.stern.nyu.edu/~aghose/ISR.pdf.

[30] Michael Riley et al., "Missed Alarms and 40 Million Stolen Credit Card Numbers: How Target Blew It," Bloomberg Businessweek, March 13, 2014, http://www.business week.com/printer/articles/189573-missed-alarms-and-40-millionstolen-credit-card-numbers-how-target-blew-it.

[31] Jon W. Burd, "Cybersecurity Developments: Does the NIST "Voluntary" Framework Portend New Requirements for Contractors," Wiley Rein LLP, 2013, http://www.wileyrein.com/publications.cfm?sp=articles&newsletter=3&id=9264.

[32] The critical sectors are chemicals, communications, commercial facilities, critical manufacturing, dams, defense industrial base, emergency services, energy, financial services, food and agriculture, government, healthcare and public health, information technology, nuclear, transportation, and water and waste water. For more information, see National Telecommunications and Information Administration, "Presidential Decision Directive 63 on Critical Infrastructure Protection," 63 Federal Register 41804-41806, August 5, 1998.

[33] ISAC Council, "Government–Private Sector Relations," January 31, 2004, http://www.isaccouncil.org/images/ Government_Private_Sector_Relations_013104.pdf.

[34] Zachary Goldfarb and Ellen Nakashima, "Lew Says Financial Industry Could Do More to Prevent Cyberattacks," Washington Post, July 16, 2014, http://www.washingtonpost.com/business/economy/lew-says-financial-industry-coulddo-more-to-prevent-cyberattacks/2014/07/16/6909e970-0d22-11e4-8341-b8072b1e7348_story.html.

[35] Joseph Straw, "Food Sector Abandons Its ISAC," Security Management, http://www.securitymanagement.com/ article/food-sector-abandons-its-isac-004590.

[36] CRS Report R43496, The Target and Other Financial Data Breaches: Frequently Asked Questions, by N. Eric Weiss and Rena S. Miller.

[37] New York State Department of Financial Services, Report on Cyber Security in the Banking Sector, May 2014, p. 4, http://www.dfs.ny.gov/about/press2014/pr 140505_ cyber_security.pdf.

[38] The White House, "Getting Serious about Information Sharing for Cybersecurity," April 10, 2014, http://www.whitehouse.gov/blog/2014/04/10/getting-serious-about-information-sharing-cybersecurity.

[39] IT-ISAC, Members, August 7 2014, http://www.it-isac.org/#!members/c1tsl.

[40] Letter from Brian Willis, president, IT-ISAC, to Dr. Melissa Hathaway, acting senior director for cyberspace, NSC, February 27, 2009, http://www.whitehouse.gov/files/documents/cyber/Willis%20Brian%20-%20IT%20ISAC%20Final%20Letter%20to%20Dr%20Hathaway.pdf.

[41] TSC Industries, Inc. v. Northway, Inc., 426 U.S. 438 (1976). For a discussion of recent controversies involving disclosure (or nondisclosure) of "material information," see Steven Davidoff Solomon, "In Corporate Disclosure, a Murky Definition of Material," New York Times, April 5, 2011, http://dealbook.nytimes.com/2011/04/05/in-corporatedisclosure-a-murky-definition-of-material/?_php=true&_type=blogs&_r=0.

[42] Jon W. Burd, "Cybersecurity Developments: Does the NIST 'Voluntary' Framework Portend New Requirements for Contractors?" Wiley Rein LLP, 2013, http://www.wileyrein.com/publications.cfm?sp=articles&newsletter=3&id= 9264.

[43] Dan Geer, "Cybersecurity as Realpolitik," keynote address at Black Hat USA 2014, Las Vegas, NV, August 6, 2014, http://geer.tinho.net/geer.blackhat.6viii14.txt.

[44] David Inserra and Paul Rosenzweig, "Cybersecurity Information Sharing: One Step towards U.S. Security, Prosperity, and Freedom in Cyberspace," Heritage Foundation, April 1, 2014, http://www.heritage.org/research/reports/ 2014/04/cybersecurity-information-sharing-one-step-toward-us-security-prosperity-and-freedom-in-cyberspace.

[45] George Akerlof, "The Market for 'Lemons': Quality Uncertainty and the Market Mechanism," Quarterly Journal of Economics, vol. 84, no. 3 (August 1970), pp. 488-500.

[46] In addition, an organization's cybersecurity depends on all the defensive measures that it has taken. A perfect antivirus program does not exist, but even if it did it would not protect against other types of attack.

[47] Federal Trade Commission v. Wyndham Worldwide Corporation, et al., Civil Action No. 13-1887 (ES) (U.S. District Court of New Jersey 2014). For CRS legal analyses of these issues see, for example, CRS Legal Sidebar WSLG947, FTC v. Wyndham Worldwide Corp.: NJ Federal District Court Upholds the FTC's Authority to Regulate Data Security as an Unfair Trade Practice, by Gina Stevens

[48] Nicole Perlroth and Elizabeth A. Harris, "Cyberattack Insurance a Challenge for Business," New York Times, June 8, 2014, http://www.nytimes.com/2014/06/09/business/cyberattack-insurance-a-challenge-for-business.html?_r=0.

[49] Ibid.

[50] In the 112th Congress, a similar bill, H.R. 3523, the Cyber Intelligence Sharing and Protection Act, also passed the House.

[51] Letter from Joel I. Klein, assistant attorney general, to Barbara Greenspan, Esq., associate general counsel, Electric Power Research Institute, October 2, 2000, http://www.justice.gov/atr/public/busreview/6614.pdf.

[52] For more information, see CRS Report WSLG480, Privacy and Civil Liberties Issues Raised by CISPA, by Andrew Nolan.

[53] Office of Management and Budget, "Statement of Administration Policy, H.R. 624 - Cyber Intelligence Sharing and Protection Act," April 16, 2013, http://www.whitehouse.gov/sites/default/files/omb/legislative/sap/113/ saphr624r_20130416.pdf.

[54] Senator Kirsten Gillibrand, "Gillibrand Introduces New Cyber-Security Legislation," press release, July 31, 2014, http://www.gillibrand.senate.gov/newsroom/press/release/gillibrand-introduces-new-cyber-security-legislation-afternew-9/11-commission-report-released-last-week-concluded-a-9/10-ability-to-protect-against-cyber-attacks.

[55] For more information on tax credits, see CRS Report R42726, The Corporate Income Tax System: Overview and Options for Reform, by Mark P. Keightley and Molly F. Sherlock and CRS Report RL32808, Overview of the Federal Tax System, by Molly F. Sherlock and Donald J. Marples.

[56] A company that has no tax liability in a year would not benefit from the tax credit.

[57] New York State Department of Financial Services, "Report on Cyber Security in the Banking Sector," May 2014, p. 4, http://www.dfs.ny.gov/about/press2014/pr140505_ cyber_ksecurity.pdf.

[58] For information on other legislation, including bills passed in previous Congresses, see CRS Report R42114, Federal Laws Relating to Cybersecurity: Overview of Major Issues, Current Laws, and Proposed Legislation, by Eric A. Fischer.

[59] For more information, see CRS Report R42475, Data Security Breach Notification Laws, by Gina Stevens and CRS Report R42474, Selected Federal Data Security Breach Legislation, by Kathleen Ann Ruane.

In: Cybersecurity and Cyber-Information Sharing ISBN: 978-1-63483-137-6
Editor: Julia M. Morgan

Chapter 3

CYBERSECURITY AND INFORMATION SHARING: COMPARISON OF H.R. 1560 AND H.R. 1731*

Eric A. Fischer

SUMMARY

It is generally recognized that effective sharing of information in cybersecurity is an important tool in the protection of information systems and their contents from unauthorized access by cybercriminals and other adversaries. Five bills on information sharing in cybersecurity have been introduced in the 114th Congress (H.R. 234, H.R. 1560, H.R. 1731, S. 456, and S. 754). The White House has also submitted a legislative proposal and issued an executive order on the topic.

In the House, H.R. 1560, the Protecting Cyber Networks Act (PCNA), was reported out of the House Permanent Select Committee on Intelligence on April 13, 2015, and H.R. 1731, the National Cybersecurity Protection Advancement Act of 2015 (NCPAA), was ordered reported by the House Committee on Homeland Security on April 14. Both bills are expected to receive floor action in the House the week of April 20. They both focus on information sharing among private entities and between them and the federal government. They address the

* This is an edited, reformatted and augmented version of a Congressional Research Service publication R43996, prepared for Members and Committees of Congress, dated April 20, 2015.

structure of the information-sharing process, issues associated with privacy and civil liberties, and liability risks for private-sector sharing, and both address some other topics in common. In addition to other provisions, the NCPAA would explicitly amend portions of the Homeland Security Act of 2002 (6 USC 101 et seq.), and the PCNA would amend parts of the National Security Act of 1947 (50 USC 3021 et seq.). Comparison of the bills reveals many similarities but also significant differences, for example in how they define terms in common such as cyber threat indicator, the roles they provide for federal agencies (especially, the Department of Homeland Security and the intelligence community), processes for nonfederal entities to share information with the federal government; processes for protecting privacy and civil liberties, uses permitted for shared information, and reporting requirements.

H.R. 1560, H.R. 1731, and the other bills would all address concerns that are commonly raised about barriers to sharing of information on threats, attacks, vulnerabilities, and other aspects of cybersecurity—both within and across sectors. Barriers to sharing have long been considered by many to be a significant hindrance to effective protection of information systems, especially those associated with critical infrastructure. Private-sector entities often claim that they are reluctant to share such information among themselves because of concerns about legal liability, antitrust violations, and protection of intellectual property and other proprietary business information. Institutional and cultural factors have also been cited—traditional approaches to security tend to emphasize secrecy and confidentiality, which would necessarily impede sharing of information. All the bills have provisions aimed at facilitating sharing of information among private-sector entities and providing protections from liability that might arise from such sharing.

While reduction or removal of such barriers may provide benefits in cybersecurity, concerns have also been raised about potential adverse impacts, especially with respect to privacy and civil liberties, and potential misuse of shared information. The legislative proposals all address many of the concerns. In general, the proposals limit the use of shared information to purposes of cybersecurity and law enforcement, and they limit government use, especially for regulatory purposes. All also include provisions to shield information shared with the federal government from public disclosure, including exemption from disclosure under the Freedom of Information Act (FOIA). All the proposals require reports to Congress on impacts of their provisions. All have provisions aimed at protecting privacy and civil liberties with respect to shared information that is not needed for cybersecurity purposes.

Most observers appear to believe that legislation on information sharing is either necessary or at least potentially beneficial—provided that appropriate protections are included—but two additional factors in particular may be worthy of consideration as the legislative proposals are debated. First, resistance to sharing of information among private-sector entities might not be substantially reduced by the actions contemplated in the legislation. Second, information sharing is only one of many facets of cybersecurity that organizations need to address to secure their systems and information.

This report compares provisions in two bills in the House of Representatives that address information sharing and related activities in cybersecurity:[1]

- H.R. 1560, the Protecting Cyber Networks Act (PCNA), as reported by the House Permanent Select Committee on Intelligence on April 13; and
- H.R. 1731, the National Cybersecurity Protection Advancement Act of 2015 (NCPAA), as ordered reported by the Committee on Homeland Security on April 14.[2]

Both bills are expected to receive floor action in the House the week of April 20. They both focus on information sharing among private entities and between them and the federal government. They address the structure of the information-sharing process, issues associated with privacy and civil liberties, and liability risks for private-sector sharing, and both address some other topics in common. In addition to other provisions, the NCPAA would explicitly amend portions of the Homeland Security Act of 2002 (6 USC 101 et seq.), and the PCNA would amend parts of the National Security Act of 1947 (50 USC 3021 et seq.).

This report consists of a discussion of those and other legislative proposals on information sharing, along with selected associated issues, followed by a side-by-side analysis of the two House bills.[3]

CURRENT LEGISLATIVE PROPOSALS

Five bills on information sharing have been introduced in the 114th Congress. The White House has also submitted a legislative proposal[4] (WHP) and issued an executive order on the topic.[5] Other proposals include the following:

- The Cyber Intelligence Sharing and Protection Act (CISPA), which passed the House in the 113th Congress, has been reintroduced as H.R. 234.
- S. 456 is an amended version of the White House proposal.[6]
- S. 754, the Cybersecurity Information Sharing Act of 2015 (CISA), from the Senate Intelligence Committee, has many similarities to a bill with the same name introduced in the 113th Congress and shares many provisions with the PCNA, although there are also significant differences between S. 754 and the PCNA.

All the bills would address concerns that are commonly raised about barriers to sharing of information on threats, attacks, vulnerabilities, and other aspects of cybersecurity—both within and across sectors. It is generally recognized that effective sharing of information is an important tool in the protection of information systems and their contents from unauthorized access by cybercriminals and other adversaries.

Barriers to sharing have long been considered by many to be a significant hindrance to effective protection of information systems, especially those associated with critical infrastructure.[7] Private-sector entities often claim that they are reluctant to share such information among themselves because of concerns about legal liability, antitrust violations, and protection of intellectual property and other proprietary business information. Institutional and cultural factors have also been cited—traditional approaches to security tend to emphasize secrecy and confidentiality, which would necessarily impede sharing of information. While reduction or removal of such barriers may provide benefits in cybersecurity, concerns have also been raised about potential adverse impacts, especially with respect to privacy and civil liberties, and potential misuse of shared information.

The legislative proposals all address many of those concerns, but they vary somewhat in emphasis and method. The NCPAA focuses on the role of the Department of Homeland Security (DHS), and in particular the National Cybersecurity and Communications Integration Center (NCCIC). The PCNA, in contrast, focuses on the role of the intelligence community (IC),[8] including authorization of the recently announced Cyber Threat Intelligence Integration Center (CTIIC). Both CISPA and CISA address roles of both DHS and the IC. The NCPAA, S. 456, and the WHP address roles of information sharing and analysis organizations (ISAOs).[9]

All of the proposals have provisions aimed at facilitating sharing of information among private-sector entities and providing protections from liability that might arise from such sharing. They vary somewhat in the kinds of private-sector entities and information covered, but almost all of them address information on both cybersecurity threats and defensive measures, the exception being S. 456 and the WHP, which cover only cyber threat indicators. In general, the proposals limit the use of shared information to purposes of cybersecurity and law enforcement, and they limit government use, especially for regulatory purposes.

All address concerns about privacy and civil liberties, although the mechanisms proposed vary to some extent, in particular the roles played by the Attorney General, the DHS Secretary, Chief Privacy Officers, the Privacy and Civil Liberties Oversight Board (PCLOB), and the Inspectors General of DHS and other agencies. All the proposals require reports to Congress on impacts of their provisions. All also include provisions to shield information shared with the federal government from public disclosure, including exemption from disclosure under the Freedom of Information Act (FOIA).

While most observers appear to believe that legislation on information sharing is either necessary or at least potentially beneficial—provided that appropriate protections are included—two caveats in particular may be worthy of consideration as the legislative proposals are developed. The first is that resistance to sharing of information among private-sector entities might not be substantially reduced by the actions contemplated in the legislation. Information received can help an entity prevent or mitigate an attack. However, there is no direct benefit associated with providing information. While the legislative proposals may reduce the risks to private-sector entities associated with providing information, none include explicit incentives to stimulate such provision. In the absence of mechanisms to balance that asymmetry, the degree to which information sharing will increase under the provisions of the various legislative proposals may be uncertain.

The second point is that information sharing is only one of many facets of cybersecurity.[10] Entities must have the resources and processes in place that are necessary for effective cybersecurity risk management. Sharing may be relatively unimportant for many organizations, especially in comparison with other cybersecurity needs.[11] In addition, most information sharing relates to imminent or near-term threats. It is not directly relevant to broader issues in cybersecurity such as education and training, workforce, acquisition, or cybercrime law, or major long-term challenges such as building security into the design of hardware and software, changing the incentive structure for cybersecurity, developing a broad consensus about cybersecurity needs and requirements, and adapting to the rapid evolution of cyberspace.

COMPARISON OF H.R. 1560 AND H.R. 1731

The remainder of the report consists of a side-by-side comparison of provisions in H.R. 1560 as reported to the House and H.R. 1731 as ordered reported. Note that the language in the bills may be subject to additional amendment before floor consideration—for example through a manager's amendment.

GLOSSARY OF ABBREVIATIONS IN THE TABLE

AG	Attorney General
CI	Critical Infrastructure
CPO	Chief Privacy Officer
CRADA	Cooperative research and development agreement
CTIIC	Cyber Threat Intelligence Integration Center
DHS	Department of Homeland Security
DNI	Director of National Intelligence
DOD	Department of Defense
DOJ	Department of Justice
HSA	Homeland Security Act
HSGAC	Senate Homeland Security and Governmental Affairs Committee
IC	Intelligence community
ICS	Industrial control system
ICS-CERT	Industrial Control System Cyber Emergency Response Team
IG	Inspector General
ISAC	Information sharing and analysis center
ISAO	Information sharing and analysis organization
MOU	Memorandum of understanding
NCCIC	National Cybersecurity and Communications Integration Center
NCPAA	National Cybersecurity Protection Advancement Act of 2015
ODNI	Office of the Director of National Intelligence
PCLOB	Privacy and Civil Liberties Oversight Board
PCNA	Protecting Cyber Networks Act
SSA	Sector-specific agency
Secretary	Secretary of Homeland Security

U.S.	United States
USC	United States Code
US-CERT	United States Computer Emergency Readiness Team
U/S-CIP	DHS Under Secretary for Cybersecurity and Infrastructure Protection

Notes on the Table

Bold formatting denotes that the identified provision is the subject of the subsequent text (e.g., (d) or Sec. 2 (a)). Numbers and names of sections, subsections, and paragraphs (except definitions) added by the bills are enclosed in single quotation marks for clarity (e.g., *'(a)'*). Entries describing provisions in a bill are summaries or paraphrases, with direct quotes enclosed in double quotation marks. Page numbers in this table refer to pages in the pdf version of this report. *Underlined* text is used in selected cases as a visual aid to highlight differences with a corresponding provision in other bills or laws that might otherwise be difficult to discern. Related provisions in different proposals are adjacent to each other. H.R. 1731 serves as the basis for comparison. The names of titles, sections, and some paragraphs are stated the first time a provision from them is discussed in the table, but only the number, to the paragraph level or higher, is used thereafter. For the PCNA, some provisions appear out of sequence in the table. In such cases, the section number is repeated before a provision from a previously cited section that appears immediately below an entry on a provision from another section. (For example, the entry Sec. 3. Authorizations for Preventing, Detecting, Analyzing, and Mitigating Cybersecurity Threats is used the first time a provision from that section is discussed, but the next appearance of one of its provisions occurs immediately after an entry for Sec. 9. Construction and Preemption and is therefore labelled Sec. 3(c)(3). That is followed immediately by a discussion of subsection (a), which is not preceded by a section number.) The entry "[Similar to NCPAA]" means that the text in that provision in the PCNA is closely similar in meaning but not identical to the corresponding provision in the NCPAA. See the "Glossary of Abbreviations in the Table" for meanings of those abbreviations.

Table 1. Side-by-Side Comparison of Two House Bills on Information Sharing

NCPAA—H.R. 1731	PCNA—H.R. 1560
"To amend the Homeland Security Act of 2002 to enhance multi-directional sharing of information related to cybersecurity risks and strengthen privacy and civil liberties protections, and for other purposes."	"To improve cybersecurity in the United States through enhanced sharing of information about cybersecurity threats, and for other purposes."
Sec. 1. Short Title National Cybersecurity Protection Advancement Act of 2015 Sec. 2. National Cybersecurity and Communications Integration Center Amends Sec. 226 of the Homeland Security Act (HSA). [Note: This is the section establishing the National Cybersecurity and Communications Integration Center added by P.L. 113-282 and is referred to in the bill as the "second section 226" to distinguish it from an identically numbered section added by P.L. 113-277.]	Sec. 1. Short Title Protecting Cyber Networks Act
(a) Definitions Adds the following:	Sec. 11. Definitions
	Agency: As in 44 USC 3502. Appropriate Federal Entities: Departments of Commerce, Defense, Energy, Homeland Security, Justice, and Treasury; and Office of the ODNI. Cybersecurity Threat: An action unprotected by the 1st Amendment to the Constitution that involves an information system and may result in unauthorized efforts to adversely impact the security, integrity, confidentiality, or availability of the system or its contents, but not including actions solely involving violations of consumer terms of service or licensing agreements.
Cyber Threat Indicator: Technical information necessary to describe or identify	Cyber Threat Indicator: Information or a physical object necessary to describe or identify
- a method for network awareness [defined below] of an information system to discern its technical vulnerabilities, if the method is known or reasonably suspected of association	- malicious reconnaissance, including

NCPAA—H.R. 1731	PCNA—H.R. 1560
with a known or suspected cybersecurity risk, including	
- communications that reasonably appear to have "the purpose of gathering technical information related to a cybersecurity risk,"	- anomalous patterns of communications that appear to have "the purpose of gathering technical information related to a cybersecurity threat or security vulnerability,"
- a method for defeating a technical or security control,	- a method of defeating a security control or exploiting a security vulnerability,
- a technical vulnerability including anomalous technical behavior that may become a vulnerability,	- a security vulnerability or anomalous activity indicating the existence of one,
- a method of causing a legitimate user of an information system or its contents to inadvertently enable defeat of a technical or operational control,	- a method of causing a legitimate user of an information system or its contents to unwittingly enable defeat of a security control or exploitation of a security vulnerability,
- a method for unauthorized remote identification, access, or use of an information system or its contents, if the method is known or reasonably suspected of association with a known or suspected cybersecurity risk, or	- "malicious cyber command and control,"
- actual or potential harm from an incident, including exfiltration of information; or	[Identical to NCPAA]
- any other cybersecurity risk attribute that cannot be used to identify specific persons believed to be unrelated to the risk, and disclosure of which is not prohibited by law	- any other cybersecurity threat attribute the disclosure of which is not prohibited by law.
- any combination of the above.	
Cybersecurity Purpose: Protecting an information system or its contents from a cybersecurity risk or incident.	Cybersecurity Purpose: Protecting (including by using defensive measures) an information system or its contents from a cybersecurity threat or security vulnerability or identifying a threat source.
Defensive Measure: An "action, device, procedure, signature, technique, or other measure" applied to an information system that "detects, prevents or mitigates a known or suspected cybersecurity risk or incident" or attributes that could help defeat security controls, but not including measures that destroy, render unusable, or	Defensive Measure: An "action, device, procedure, technique, or other measure" executed on an information system or its contents that "prevents or mitigates a known or suspected cybersecurity threat or security vulnerability."

Table 1. (Continued)

NCPAA—H.R. 1731	PCNA—H.R. 1560
substantially harm an information system not operated by that entity or by another entity that consented to such actions.	
	Federal Entity: A US department or agency, or any component thereof. Information System: As in 44 USC 3502. Local Government: A political subdivision of a state. Malicious Cyber Command and Control: "A method for unauthorized remote identification of, access to, or use of an information system" or its contents. Malicious Reconnaissance: A method, associated with a known or suspected cybersecurity threat, for probing or monitoring an information system to discern its vulnerabilities.
Network Awareness:	Monitor:
Scanning, identifying, acquiring, monitoring, logging, or analyzing the contents of an information system.	Scanning, identifying, acquiring, or otherwise possessing the contents of an information system.
	Non-Federal Entity: A private or governmental entity that is not federal, but not including foreign powers as defined in 50 USC 1801.
Private Entity: A nonfederal entity that is an individual, nonfederal government utility, or	Private Entity: A person, nonfederal government utility, or
private group, organization, proprietorship, partnership, trust, cooperative, corporation, or other commercial or nonprofit entity , including personnel.	[Identical to NCPAA] including personnel, but not including a foreign power as defined in 50 USC 1801.
	Real Time: Automated, machine-to-machine system processing of cyber threat indicators where the occurrence and "reporting or recording" of an event are "as simultaneous as technologically and operationally practicable."
Security Control: The management, operational, and technical controls used to protect an information system and its contents against unauthorized attempts to adversely	Security Control: The management, operational, and technical controls used to protect an information system and its contents against unauthorized attempts to

NCPAA—H.R. 1731	PCNA—H.R. 1560
affect their confidentiality, integrity, or availability.	adversely impact their confidentiality, integrity, or availability.
	Security Vulnerability: "Any attribute of hardware, software, process, or procedure that could enable or facilitate the defeat of a security control."
Sharing: "Providing, receiving, and disseminating."	
	Tribal: As in 25 USC 450b.
(b) Amendment Specifies tribal governments, private entities, and ISACs as appropriate members of the NCCIC in DHS.	
Sec. 3. Information Sharing Structure and Processes Amends Sec. 226 of the HSA.	Sec. 2. Sharing of Cyber Threat Indicators and Defensive Measures by the Federal Government With Non-federal Entities (a) In General Amends Title I of the National Security Act of 1947 by adding a new section. 'Sec. 111. Sharing of Cyber Threat Indicators and Defensive Measures by the Federal Government With Non-Federal Entities' '(a) Sharing by the Federal Government'
(1) revises the functions of the NCCIC by specifying that it is the "lead" federal civilian interface for information sharing, adding "cyber threat indicators" and "defensive measures" to the subjects it addresses, and expanding its functions to include	'(1)' requires the DNI, in consultation with the heads of other appropriate federal entities, to develop and promulgate procedures consistent with protection of classified information, intelligence sources and methods, and privacy and civil liberties, for timely sharing of classified cyber threat indicators and declassified indicators and information with relevant nonfederal entities, and sharing of information about imminent or ongoing cybersecurity threats to such entities to prevent and mitigate adverse impacts.
- providing information and recommendations on information sharing, - in consultation with other appropriate agencies, collaborating with international partners, including on enhancing "the security and resilience of the global cybersecurity ecosystem," and	

Table 1. (Continued)

NCPAA—H.R. 1731	PCNA—H.R. 1560
- sharing "cyber threat indicators, defensive measures," and information on cybersecurity risks and incidents with federal and nonfederal entities, including across critical-infrastructure (CI) sectors and with fusion centers. [Note: See also the provisions on the CTIIC in H.R. 1560, p. 10.] - notify the Secretary, the HSC, and the HSGAC of significant violations of privacy and civil liberties protections under 'Sec. 226(i)(6),' - promptly notifying nonfederal entities that have shared information known to be in error or in contravention to section requirements, - participating in DHS-run exercises, and	
	'(2)' requires that the procedures incorporate existing information-sharing mechanisms of federal and nonfederal entities, including ISACs, as much as possible, and include methods to promote efficient granting of security clearances to appropriate representatives of nonfederal entities.
(2) expands NCCIC membership to include the following [Note: all are existing entities]: - an entity that collaborates with state and local governments on risks and incidents and has a voluntary information sharing relationship with the NCCIC, - the US-CERT for collaboratively addressing, responding to, providing technical assistance upon request on, and coordinating information about and timely sharing of threat indicators, defensive measures, analysis, or information about cybersecurity risks and incidents, - the ICS-CERT to coordinate with ICS owners and operators, provide training on ICS cybersecurity, and timely share information about indicators, defensive measures, or cybersecurity risks and incidents of ICS, - the "National Coordinating Center for	

NCPAA—H.R. 1731	PCNA—H.R. 1560
Communications to coordinate the protection, response, and recovery of emergency communications," and - "an entity that coordinates with small and medium-sized businesses." (3) adds "cyber threat indicators" and "defensive measures" to the subjects covered in the principles of operation of the NCCIC, requires that information be shared as appropriate with small and medium-sized businesses, specifies that information be guarded against disclosure, and stipulates that the NCCIC must work with the DHS CPO to ensure that the NCCIC follows privacy and civil liberties policies and procedures under 'Sec. 226(i)(6)'; (4) adds new subsections to Sec. 226 of the HSA:	
'(g) Rapid Automated Sharing'	
'(1)' requires the DHS U/S-CIP to develop capabilities, in coordination with stakeholders and based as appropriate on existing standards and approaches in the information technology industry, that support and advance automated and timely sharing of threat indicators and defensive measures to and from the NCCIC and with SSAs for each CI sector in accordance with 'Sec. 226(h).'. '(2)' requires the U/S-CIP to report to Congress twice per year on the status and progress of that capability until it is fully implemented. '(h) Sector Specific Agencies' Requires the Secretary to collaborate with relevant CI sectors and heads of appropriate federal agencies to recognize each CI SSA designated as of March 25, 2015, in the DHS National Infrastructure Protection Plan. Designates the Secretary as SSA head for each sector for which DHS is the SSA. Requires the Secretary to coordinate with relevant SSAs to - support CI sector security and resilience activities, - provide knowledge, expertise, and assistance	ensure the capability of real-time sharing consistent with protection of classified information. [Note: 'Sec. 111(b)(2)' requires procedures to ensure such sharing—see p. 10.]

Table 1. (Continued)

NCPAA—H.R. 1731	PCNA—H.R. 1560
on request, and - support timely sharing of threat indicators and defensive measures with the NCCIC.	
	[Note: For other provisions of 'Sec. 111(a)(2)', see pp. 14 and 17.] '(b) Definitions' Defines the following terms by reference to Sec. 11 of the bill: Appropriate Federal Entities, Cyber Threat Indicator, Defensive Measure, Federal Entity, and Non-Federal Entity. (b) Submittal to Congress Requires that the procedures developed by the DNI be submitted to Congress within 90 days of enactment of the bill. (c) Table of Contents Amendment Revises the table of contents of the National Security Act of 1947 to reflect the addition of 'Sec. 111'. Sec. 4. Sharing of Cyber Threat Indicators and Defensive Measures With Appropriate Federal Entities Other Than the Department of Defense or the National Security Agency (a) Requirement for Policies and Procedures (1) Adds new subsections to 'Sec. 111' of the National Security Act of 1947
'(i) Voluntary Information Sharing Procedures'	'(b) Policies and Procedures for Sharing with the Appropriate Federal Entities Other Than the Department of Defense or the National Security Agency' '(1)' requires the President to develop and submit to Congress policies and procedures for federal receipt of cyber threat indicators and defensive measures.
'(1)' permits voluntary information-sharing relationships for cybersecurity purposes between the NCCIC and nonfederal entities but prohibits requiring such an agreement.	

NCPAA—H.R. 1731	PCNA—H.R. 1560
Permits the NCCIC to terminate an agreement for repeated, intentional violation of the terms of '(h).' Permits the Secretary to deny an agreement for national security reasons. '(2)' permits the relationship to be established through a standard agreement for nonfederal entities not requiring specific terms. Stipulates negotiated agreements with DHS where appropriate. Permits other agreements between the NCCIC and consenting nonfederal entities. Stipulates that any agreement in effect prior to enactment of the bill will be deemed in compliance with requirements in '(h).'Requires that those agreements include "relevant privacy protections as in effect under Cooperative Research and Development Agreement for Cybersecurity Information Sharing and Collaboration, as of December 31st 2014."	
	'(2)' requires that they be developed in accordance with the privacy and civil liberties guidelines under Sec. 4(b) of the bill, ensure - real-time sharing of indicators from nonfederal entities with appropriate federal entities except DOD, - receipt without delay except for good cause, and - provision to all relevant federal entities, - audit capability, and - appropriate sanctions for federal personnel who knowingly and willfully use shared information other than in accordance with the bill. (2) requires that an interim version of the policies and procedures be submitted to Congress within 90 days of enactment of the bill, and the final version within 180 days. (c) National Cyber Threat Intelligence Integration Center (1) Adds a new section to the National Security Act of 1947.

Table 1. (Continued)

NCPAA—H.R. 1731	PCNA—H.R. 1560
	'Sec. 119b. Cyber Threat Intelligence Integration Center' '(a) Establishment' Establishes the CTIIC within the ODNI. '(b) Director' Creates a director for the CTIIC, to be appointed by the DNI. '(c) Primary Missions' Specifies the missions of the CTIIC with respect to cyberthreat intelligence as - serving as the primary federal organization for analyzing and integrating it, - ensuring full access and support of appropriate agencies to activities and analysis, - disseminating analysis to the President, appropriate agencies, and Congress, - coordinating agency activities, and - conducting strategic federal planning. '(d) Limitations' Requires that the CTIIC - have no more than 50 permanent positions, - may not augment staff above that limit in carrying out its primary missions, and - be located in a building owned and operated by an element of the IC, (4) revises the table of contents of the National Security Act of 1947. Sec. 3. Authorizations for Preventing, Detecting, Analyzing, and Mitigating Cybersecurity Threats
'(3) Information Sharing Authorization' Permits nonfederal entities to share, for cybersecurity purposes, cyber threat indicators, and defensive measures, from their own information systems or those of other entities upon written consent, with other nonfederal entities or the NCCIC,	(c) Authorization for Sharing or Receiving Cyber Threat Indicators or Defensive Measures (1) permits nonfederal entities to share, for cybersecurity purposes and consistent with privacy requirements under (d)(2), lawfully obtained cyber threat indicators or defensive measures with other nonfederal entities or appropriate

NCPAA—H.R. 1731	PCNA—H.R. 1560
	federal entities except DOD,
notwithstanding any other provision of law, except that recipients must comply with lawful restrictions on sharing and use imposed by the source.	[Similar to NCPAA]. (d) Protection and Use of Information
Requires reasonable efforts by nonfederal and federal entities, prior to sharing, to safeguard personally identifying information from unintended disclosure or unauthorized access or acquisition and remove such information where it is reasonably believed when it is shared to be unrelated to a cybersecurity risk or incident.	(2) requires reasonable efforts by nonfederal entities, before sharing a threat indicator, to remove information reasonably believed to be personal or personally identifying of a specific person not directly related to a cybersecurity threat, or implement a technical capability for removing such information.
	Sec. 9. Construction and Preemption (f) Information Sharing Relationships
Stipulates that nothing in '(3)' - limits or modifies an existing information sharing relationship or prohibits or requires a new one,	Stipulates that nothing in the bill -(1) limits or modifies an existing information sharing relationship or (2) prohibits or requires a new one, Sec. 3(c)(3) stipulates that nothing in (c) - authorizes information sharing other than as provided in (c), - permits unauthorized sharing of classified information, - authorizes federal surveillance of any person, - prohibits a federal entity, at the request of a nonfederal entity, from technical discussion of threat indicators and defensive measures and assistance with vulnerabilities and threat mitigation, - prohibits an authorized nonfederal entity from sharing indicators or defensive measures with DOD, or - limits otherwise lawful activity, or - limits otherwise lawful activity.
- impacts or modifies existing procedures for reporting criminal activity to appropriate law enforcement authorities, or participating in an investigation. Requires the U/S-CIP to coordinate with stakeholders to develop and implement policies	

Table 1. (Continued)

NCPAA—H.R. 1731	PCNA—H.R. 1560
and procedures to coordinate disclosures of vulnerabilities as practicable and consistent with relevant international industry standards.	
'(4) Network Awareness Authorization'	(a) Authorization for Private-Sector Defensive Monitoring (1) permits private entities, notwithstanding any other provision of law, to monitor, for cybersecurity purposes, [Similar to NCPAA], [Similar to NCPAA], or [Similar to NCPAA]. (2) Stipulates that nothing in (a) - authorizes monitoring other than as provided in the bill, -limits otherwise lawful activity, or - authorizes federal surveillance of any person.
permits nonfederal, nongovernment entities, notwithstanding any other provision of law, to conduct network awareness, for cybersecurity purposes and to protect rights or property, of - its own information systems, - with written consent, information systems of a nonfederal or federal entity, or - the contents of such systems. Stipulates that nothing in '(4)' - authorizes network awareness other than as provided in the section, or - limits otherwise lawful activity,	
'(5) Defensive Measure Authorization'	(b) Authorization for Operation of Defensive Measures
permits nonfederal, nongovernment entities to operate defensive measures, for cybersecurity purposes and to protect rights or property, that are applied to - its own information systems, - with written consent, information systems of a nonfederal or federal entity, or - the contents of such systems, notwithstanding any other provision of law, except that measures may not be used except as authorized in the section, and '(5)' does not limit otherwise lawful activity.	(1) permits private entities to operate defensive measures, for cybersecurity purposes and to protect rights or property, that are operated on and the effects of which are limited to [Similar to NCPAA], or [Similar to NCPAA], (3) notwithstanding any other provision of law, except that measures may not be used except as authorized in (b), and (b) does not limit otherwise lawful activity. (2) stipulates that (1) does not authorize operation of defensive measures that intentionally or recklessly destroy, render wholly or partly unusable or inaccessible, substantially harm, or initiate a new action, process, or procedure on an information system or its contents not owned by either the private entity operating the measure or a nonfederal or federal entity that provided written authorization to that private entity. (e) No Right or Benefit Stipulates that

NCPAA—H.R. 1731	PCNA—H.R. 1560
	sharing of indicators with a nonfederal entity creates no right or benefit to similar information by any nonfederal entity.
'(6) Privacy and Civil Liberties Protections'	Sec. 4 (b) Privacy and Civil Liberties
Requires the U/S-CIP, in coordination with the DHS CPO and	(1) requires the AG, in consultation with appropriate federal
Chief Civil Rights and Civil Liberties Officer,	agency heads and agency privacy and civil liberties officers,
to establish and review annually policies and procedures on	to develop and review periodically guidelines on privacy and
information shared with the NCCIC under the section.	civil liberties to govern federal handling of cyber threat
	indicators obtained through the bill's provisions.
Requires that they apply only to DHS, consistent with the need for timely protection of information systems from and mitigation of cybersecurity risks and incidents, the policies and procedures	(2) requires that, consistent with the need for protection of information systems and threat mitigation, the guidelines
- be consistent with DHS Fair Information Practice Principles,	- be consistent with Fair Information Practice Principles in the White House National Strategy for Trusted Identities in Cyberspace [Note: The two versions of the principles are identical, except that the DHS version applies the principles to DHS whereas the White House document applies them to "organizations"],
- "reasonably limit, to the extent practicable, receipt, retention, use, and disclosure of cybersecurity threat indicators and defensive measures associated with specific persons" not needed for timely protection of systems and networks,	- limit receipt, retention, use, and dissemination of cybersecurity threat indicators containing personal information of or identifying specific persons, including by establishing processes for prompt destruction of information known not to be directly related to uses under the bill, and notification of recipients that indicators may be used only for cybersecurity purposes, and setting limitations on retention of indicators,
- minimize impacts on privacy and civil liberties,	- limit impacts on privacy and civil liberties of federal activities
	under the bill, including
- provide data integrity through prompt removal and	guidelines for removal of personal and personally identifying

Table 1. (Continued)

NCPAA—H.R. 1731	PCNA—H.R. 1560
destruction of obsolete or erroneous personal information	information handled by federal entities under the bill,
unrelated to the information shared and retained by the	
NCCIC in accordance with this section,	
- include requirements to safeguard from unauthorized access	- include requirements to safeguard from unauthorized access
or acquisition cyber threat indicators and defensive measures	or acquisition cyber threat indicators
retained by the NCCIC,	
identifying specific persons, including proprietary or business-	containing personal information of or identifying specific
sensitive information,	persons,
- protect the confidentiality of cyber threat indicators and	
defensive measures associated with specific persons, to the	
greatest extent practicable,	
- ensure that relevant constitutional, legal, and privacy	- be consistent with other applicable provisions of law,
protections are observed.	
	- include procedures to notify entities if a federal entity
	receiving information knows that it is not a cyber threat
	indicator,
	- include steps to ensure that dissemination of indicators is
	consistent with the protection of classified and other sensitive
	national security information.
Stipulates that the U/S-CIP may consult with NIST in	
developing the policies and procedures.	
Requires the DHS CPO and the Officer for Civil Rights and	Requires the AG to submit to Congress
Civil Liberties, in consultation with the PCLOB, to submit to	
appropriate congressional committees	
the policies and procedures within 180 days of enactment and	interim guidelines within 90 days of enactment and final

NCPAA—H.R. 1731	PCNA—H.R. 1560
annually thereafter.	guidelines within 180 days.
Requires the U/S-CIP, in consultation with the PCLOB and the DHS CPO and Chief Civil Rights and Civil Liberties Officer, to ensure public notice of and access to the policies and procedures. Requires the DHS CPO to - monitor implementation of the policies and procedures, - submit to Congress an annual review on their effectiveness, - work with the U/S-CIP to carry out provisions in '(c)' on notification about violations of privacy and civil liberties policies and procedures and about information that is erroneous or in contravention of section requirements, - regularly review and update impact assessments as appropriate to ensure that all relevant protections are followed, and	
	'Sec. 111(a)(2)' requires that procedures for sharing developed by the DNI include methods to notify nonfederal entities that have received information from a federal entity known to be in error or in contravention to bill requirements.
- ensure appropriate sanctions for DHS personnel who knowingly and willfully conduct unauthorized activities under the section.	Sec. 4(b)(2) requires that the AG's guidelines include appropriate sanctions for federal activities in contravention of them. [Note: The provision does not specify whether these sanctions are limited to violation of requirements for safeguarding information or the guidelines as a whole.], Sec. 7. Oversight of Government Activities (b) Reports on Privacy and Civil Liberties.
Requires the DHS IG, in consultation with the PCLOB and IGs of other agencies receiving shared indicators or defensive measures from	(2) requires the IGs of DHS, the IC, DOJ, and DOD to jointly submit a biennial report to Congress on

Table 1. (Continued)

NCPAA—H.R. 1731	PCNA—H.R. 1560
the NCCIC, to submit a report to HSC and HSGAC within two years of enactment and periodically thereafter reviewing such information, including - receipt, use, and dissemination of cybersecurity indicators and defensive measures shared with federal entities under the section, - information on NCCIC use of such information for purposes other than cybersecurity, - types of information shared with the NCCIC, - actions taken by NCCIC based on shared information; - metrics to determine impacts of sharing on privacy and civil liberties, - a list of federal agencies receiving the information, - identification of inappropriate stovepiping of shared information, - recommendations for improvements or modifications to sharing under the section.	- receipt, use, and dissemination of cybersecurity indicators and defensive measures shared with federal entities under the bill, - types of indicators shared with federal entities, - actions taken by federal entities as a result of receiving shared indicators, - a list of federal entities receiving the indicators, - identification of inappropriate barriers to sharing information, - recommendations for improvements or modifications to authorities under the bill. Requires that the reports be submitted in unclassified form but permits a classified annex. Requires public availability of unclassified parts of the reports.
Requires the DHS CPO and Chief Civil Rights and Civil Liberties Officer, in consultation with the PCLOB, the DHS IG, and senior privacy and civil liberties officers of each federal agency receiving indicators or defensive measures shared with the NCCIC, to	(1) requires the PCLOB to
submit a biennial report to Congress assessing impacts on privacy and civil liberties of federal activities under '(6)', including recommendations to minimize or mitigate such impacts.	submit a biennial report to Congress and the President assessing impacts of activities under the bill on and sufficiency of policies, procedures, and guidelines in addressing concerns about privacy and civil liberties, including recommendations for improvements or modifications to authorities under the bill.
	Requires that the reports be submitted in unclassified form but permits a classified annex.
	Requires public availability of unclassified parts of the reports.
	(a) Biennial Report on Implementation

NCPAA—H.R. 1731	PCNA—H.R. 1560
	Adds to 'Sec. 111' of the National Security Act
	'(c) Biennial Report on Implementation'
	'(1)' requires the DNI to submit a report to Congress on implementation of the bill, '(2)' within one year of enactment and '(1)' at least biennially thereafter, including
	- review of types of indicators shared with the federal government,
	- the degree to which such information may impact privacy and civil liberties of specific persons, along with quantitative and qualitative assessment of such impacts and adequacy of federal efforts to reduce them,
	- assessment of sufficiency of policies, procedures, and guidelines to ensure effective and responsible sharing under Sec. 4 of the PCNA,
	- sufficiency of procedures under Sec. 3 for timely sharing,
	- appropriateness of classification of indicators and accounting of security clearances authorized,
	- federal actions taken based on shared indicators, including appropriateness of subsequent use or dissemination under the bill,
	- description of any significant federal violations of the requirements of the bill, including assessments of all reports of federal personnel misusing information provided under the bill and all disciplinary actions taken, and
	- a summary of the number and types of nonfederal entities receiving classified indicators from the federal government and
	evaluation of risks and benefits of such sharing.
	'(3)' permits reports to include recommendations for improvements or modifications to authorities and processes

Table 1. (Continued)

NCPAA—H.R. 1731	PCNA—H.R. 1560
	under the bill.
	'(4)' requires that the reports be submitted in unclassified form but permits a classified annex.
	'(5)' requires public availability of unclassified parts of the reports.
'(7) Uses and Protection of Information'	Sec. 3. Authorizations for Preventing, Detecting, Analyzing, and Mitigating Cybersecurity Threats
	(d) Protection and Use of Information
[Nonfederal Entities]	
Permits a nonfederal, nongovernment entity that shares indicators or defensive measures with the NCCIC to	(3) permits a nonfederal entity [Note: including government entities], for a cybersecurity purpose, to
use, retain, or disclose indicators and defensive measures, solely for cybersecurity purposes.	use indicators or defensive measure shared or received under (d) to monitor or operate a defensive measure on its own information systems or those of other nonfederal or federal entities upon written authorization from them, with
Requires reasonable efforts prior to sharing to safeguard personally identifying information from unintended disclosure and unauthorized access or acquisition, and remove such information where it is reasonably believed when shared to be unrelated to a cybersecurity risk or incident.	[See (2), p. 11, describing requirements for removal of personal information].
Requires compliance with appropriate restrictions on subsequent disclosure or retention placed by a federal or nonfederal entity on indicators or defensive measures disclosed to other entities.	further use, retention, or sharing subject to lawful restrictions by the sharing entity or otherwise applicable provisions of law.
Stipulates that the information shall be deemed voluntarily shared.	
Requires implementation and utilization of security controls to protect against unauthorized access or acquisition.	(1) requires implementation of appropriate security controls to protect against unauthorized access or acquisition.
Prohibits use of such information to gain an unfair competitive advantage.	
[Federal Entities]	Sec. 4(d) Information Shared with or Provided to the Federal Government

NCPAA—H.R. 1731	PCNA—H.R. 1560
Permits federal entities receiving indicators or defensive measures from the NCCIC or otherwise under the section to use, retain, or further disclose it solely for - cybersecurity purposes.	(5) permits federal entities or personnel receiving indicators or defensive measures under the bill to, consistent with otherwise applicable provisions of federal law, use, retain, or disclose it solely for - a cybersecurity purpose, - responding to, prosecuting, or otherwise preventing or mitigating threats of death or serious bodily harm or offenses arising out of such threats, - responding to serious threats to minors, including sexual exploitation and threats to physical safety, and - preventing, investigating, disrupting, or prosecuting fraud and identity theft, espionage and censorship, protection of trade secrets, and serious violent felonies. Prohibits federal disclosure, retention, or use for any purpose not permitted under (5).
Requires reasonable efforts prior to sharing to safeguard personally identifying information from unintended disclosure and unauthorized access or acquisition, and remove such information where it is reasonably believed when shared to be unrelated to a cybersecurity risk or incident.	Stipulates that the policies, procedures, and guidelines in Sec. 4(a) [on provision of information to the federal government] and (b) [on privacy and civil liberties] of the bill apply to such information. 'Sec. 111(a)(2)' requires that procedures for sharing developed by the DNI include methods for federal entities to assess, prior to sharing, whether an indicator contains information known to be personal or personally identifying of a specific person and to remove such information, or to implement a technical capability to do so.
Stipulates that the indicators and defensive measures shall be deemed voluntarily shared. Requires implementation and utilization of security controls to protect against unauthorized access or acquisition.	Sec. 4(d)(3) stipulates that the information shall be deemed voluntarily shared. 'Sec. 111(a)(2)' requires that procedures for sharing developed by the DNI include requirements for federal entities to implement security controls to protect against unauthorized access to or acquisition of shared information. Sec. 9(a) Prohibition of Surveillance

Table 1. (Continued)

NCPAA—H.R. 1731	PCNA—H.R. 1560
Prohibits use in surveillance or collection activities to track an	Stipulates that the bill does not authorize DOD or any
individual's personally identifiable information.	element of the IC to target a person for surveillance.
Stipulates that the information is exempt from disclosure	Sec. 4(d)(3) [Similar to NCPAA], and
under 5 USC 552 [the Freedom of Information Act (FOIA)]	
or nonfederal disclosure laws and withheld, without	
discretion, from the public under 5 USC 552(3)(B).	
	exempt from disclosure under nonfederal disclosure laws, except for those requiring disclosure in criminal prosecutions.
Prohibits use for regulatory purposes.	[Note: No specific corresponding prohibition, but Sec. 4(d)(5) above prohibits federal disclosure, retention, or use for any purpose other than those specified in the paragraph.]
Specifies that there is no waiver of applicable privilege or	(1) [Similar to NCPAA].
protection under law, including trade-secret protection;	
Requires that the information be considered the commercial, financial, and proprietary information of the nonfederal entity when so designated by it.	(2) requires that, consistent with Sec. 3(c)(2), the information be considered the commercial, financial, and proprietary information of the originating nonfederal source, when so designated by such source or nonfederal entity acting with written authorization from it.
Stipulates that the information is not subject to judicial doctrine or rules of federal entities on ex-parte communications.	(4) [Similar to NCPAA]
[Nonfederal Government Entities] Permits indicators or defensive measures shared under the section with state, local, and tribal government to be used, retained, or further disclosed solely for cybersecurity purposes.	[Note: See also Nonfederal Entities, p. 16] Sec. 3(d)(4) permits state, local, and tribal government entities to use shared cyber threat indicators for cybersecurity purposes, responding to, prosecuting, or otherwise preventing or mitigating threats of death or serious bodily harm or

NCPAA—H.R. 1731	PCNA—H.R. 1560
	offenses arising out of such threats, or responding to serious threats to minors, including sexual exploitation and threats to physical safety.
Requires reasonable efforts prior to sharing to safeguard personally identifying information from unintended disclosure and unauthorized access or acquisition, and remove such information where it is reasonably believed when shared to be unrelated to a cybersecurity risk or incident.	[See (2), p. 11, describing requirements for removal of personal information].
Stipulates that the information be considered "commercial, financial, and proprietary" if so designated by the provider.	[Note: Sec. 3(d)(3) stipulates that further use, retention, or sharing of information received by a nonfederal entity is subject to lawful restrictions by the sharing entity or otherwise applicable provisions of law. See Nonfederal Entities, p. 16.]
Stipulates that the indicators and defensive measures shall be deemed voluntarily shared.	Stipulates that such shared indicators be deemed voluntarily shared and exempt from disclosure, and
Requires implementation and utilization of security controls to protect against unauthorized access or acquisition.	
Exempts the information from disclosure under nonfederal disclosure laws or regulations.	exempts the shared indicators from disclosure under nonfederal disclosure laws or regulations, except as required in criminal prosecutions.
Prohibits use for regulation of lawful activities of nonfederal entities.	
'(8) Liability Exemptions'	Sec. 6. Protection from Liability
	(a) Monitoring of Information Systems
States that "no cause of action shall lie or be maintained in any court" against nonfederal, nongovernment entities for conducting network awareness under '(4)' conducted under Sec. 3(a) in accordance with the section or	States that "no cause of action shall lie or be maintained in any court" against private entities for monitoring information systems under Sec. 3(a) conducted in good faith in accordance with the bill or
	(b) Sharing or Receipt of Cyber Threat Indicators
for sharing indicators or defensive measures under '(3),' or a failure to act if sharing is done in accordance with the section.	for information sharing under Sec. 3(c) in accordance with the bill or a good-faith failure to act if sharing is done in accordance with the bill.
stipulates that nothing in the section	(c)(1) stipulates that nothing in the section

Table 1. (Continued)

NCPAA—H.R. 1731	PCNA—H.R. 1560
- requires dismissal of a cause of action against a nonfederal, nongovernment entity that engages in willful misconduct in the course of activities under the section.	- requires dismissal of a cause of action against a nonfederal entity that engages in willful misconduct in the course of activities under the bill, or
- undermines or limits availability of otherwise applicable common law or statutory defenses.	[Identical to NCPAA]
Establishes the burden of proof as clear and convincing evidence from the plaintiff of injury-causing gross negligence or willful misconduct,	(2) [Similar to NCPAA]
Defines willful misconduct as an act or omission taken intentionally to achieve a wrongful purpose, knowingly without justification, and in disregard of risk of highly probable harm that outweighs any benefit.	(3) [Similar to NCPAA].
'(9) Federal Government Liability for Violations of Restrictions on the Use and Protection of Voluntarily Shared Information'	Sec. 5. Federal Government Liability for Violations of Privacy or Civil Liberties
	(a) In General
Makes the federal government liable to injured persons for intentional or willful violation of restrictions on federal disclosure and use under 'Sec. 226', with minimum damages of $1,000 plus	Makes the federal government liable to injured persons for intentional or willful violation of privacy and civil liberties guidelines under Sec. 4(b), with minimum damages of $1,000 plus
reasonable attorney fees as determined by the court and other reasonable litigation costs in any case under (a) where "the complainant has substantially prevailed."	[Identical to NCPAA]
	(b) Venue
Stipulates the federal district courts where the case may be brought as the one in which the complainant resides or the principal place of business is located, the District of Columbia,	[Identical to NCPAA]
or	
where the federal department or agency that disclosed the information is located.	where the federal department or agency that violated the guidelines is located.
	(c) Statute of Limitations
Sets the statute of limitations at two years from the date of violation of restrictions in provisions on information-sharing authorization ('(h)(3),') privacy and civil	Sets the statute of limitations at two years from the date of violation of guidelines on privacy and civil liberties.

NCPAA—H.R. 1731	PCNA—H.R. 1560
liberties ('(h)(6),') or federal use and protection of information ('(h)(7)(B)').	
	(d) Exclusive Cause of Action.
Sets action under '(h)' as the exclusive remedy for violation of restrictions under '(h)(3),' '(h)(6),' or '(h)(7)(B)'.	Sets action under (d) as the exclusive remedy for federal violations under the bill.
'(10) Anti-Trust Exemption'	
Exempts nonfederal entities from violation of antitrust laws for sharing indicators or defensive measures or providing assistance for cybersecurity purposes, provided that the action is taken to assist with preventing, investigating, or mitigating a cybersecurity risk or incident. Prohibits specified monopolistic activities such as price-fixing.	
'(11) Construction and Preemption'	Sec. 9(b) Otherwise Lawful Disclosures
Stipulates that the section does not limit or prohibit otherwise lawful disclosures or participation in an investigation by a nonfederal entity of information to any other federal or nonfederal entity.	Stipulates that the bill does not limit or prohibit otherwise lawful disclosures by a nonfederal entity of information to any other federal or nonfederal entity, or any otherwise lawful use by a federal entity, whether or not the disclosures duplicate those made under the bill.
	(c) Whistle Blower Protections
Stipulates that the section does not prohibit or limit disclosures protected under 5 USC 2302(b)(8), 5 USC 7211, 10 USC 1034, 50 USC 3234, or similar provisions of federal or state law.	Stipulates that the bill does not prohibit or limit disclosures protected under 5 USC 2302(b)(8), 5 USC 7211, 10 USC 1034, or similar provisions of federal or state law.
	(e) Relationship to Other Laws
Stipulates that the section does not affect any requirements under other provisions of law for nonfederal entities providing information to federal entities.	Stipulates that the bill does not affect any requirements under other provisions of law for nonfederal entities providing information to federal entities.
	(g) Preservation of Contractual Obligations and Rights
Stipulates that the section does not change contractual relationships between nonfederal entities or them and federal entities or abrogate trade-secret or intellectual property rights.	Stipulates that the bill does not change contractual relationships between nonfederal entities or them and federal entities, or abrogate trade-secret or intellectual property rights.
	(h) Anti-Tasking Restriction
Stipulates that the section does not permit the federal government to require nonfederal	Stipulates that the bill does not permit the federal government to require nonfederal

Table 1. (Continued)

NCPAA—H.R. 1731	PCNA—H.R. 1560
entities to provide it with information, or condition sharing of indicators or defensive measures on provision by such entities of indicators or defensive measures, or condition award of grants, contracts, or purchases on such provision.	entities to provide it with information, or condition sharing of indicators on provision of indicators, or condition award of grants, contracts, or purchases on such provision.
	(i) No Liability for Non-Participation
Stipulates that the section does not create liabilities for any nonfederal entities that choose not to engage in the voluntary activities authorized in the section.	Stipulates that the bill does not create liabilities for any nonfederal entities that choose not to engage in the voluntary activities authorized in the bill.
	(j) Use and Retention of Information
Stipulates that the section does not authorize or modify existing federal authority to retain and use information shared under the bill for uses other than those permitted under the section.	Stipulates that the bill does not authorize or modify existing federal authority to retain and use information shared under the bill for uses other than those permitted under the bill.
Stipulates that the section does not restrict or condition sharing for cybersecurity purposes among nonfederal entities or require sharing by them with the NCCIC.	
	(k) Federal Preemption
Specifies that the section supersedes state and local laws relating to its provisions	(1) specifies that the bill supersedes state and local laws relating to its provisions.
	(2) stipulates that the bill does not supersede state and local laws on use of authorized law enforcement practices and procedures.
Requires the Secretary to develop policies and procedures for direct reporting by the NCCIC Director of significant risks and incidents. Requires the Secretary to build on existing mechanisms to promote public awareness about the importance of securing information systems. Requires a report from the Secretary within 180 days of enactment to HSC and HSGAC on efforts to bolster collaboration on cybersecurity with international partners. Requires the Secretary, within 60 days of enactment, to publicly disseminate information	

NCPAA—H.R. 1731	PCNA—H.R. 1560
about ways of sharing information with the NCCIC, including enhanced outreach to CI owners and operators.	
	(d) Protection of Sources and Methods Stipulates that the bill does not affect federal enforcement actions on classified information or conduct of authorized law-enforcement or intelligence activities, or modify the authority of the President or federal entities to protect and control dissemination of classified information, sources and methods, and U.S. national security.
Sec. 4. Information Sharing and Analysis Organizations	
Amends Sec. 212 of the HSA to	
(1) broaden the functions of ISAOs to include cybersecurity risk and incident information beyond that relating to critical infrastructure, and	
(2) add by reference the definitions of cybersecurity risk and incident in 6 USC 148(a).	
Sec. 5. Streamlining of Department of Homeland Security Cybersecurity and Infrastructure Protection Organization	
(a) Cybersecurity and Infrastructure Protection Directorate	
Renames the DHS National Protection and Programs Directorate as the Cybersecurity and Infrastructure Protection. [Sic.]	
(b) Senior Leadership of the Cybersecurity and Infrastructure Protection Directorate	
Provides a specific title for the undersecretary in charge of critical infrastructure protection as U/S-CIP. Also adds two deputy undersecretaries, one for cybersecurity and the other for infrastructure protection. Does not require new appointments for current officeholders and specifies that appointment of the undersecretaries does not require Senate confirmation.	
(c) Report	
Requires a report to HSC and HSGAC from	

Table 1. (Continued)

NCPAA—H.R. 1731	PCNA—H.R. 1560
the U/S-CIP within 90 days of enactment on the feasibility of becoming an operational component of DHS, If that is determined to be the best option for mission fulfillment, requires submission of a legislative proposal and implementation plan. Also requires that the report include plans for more effective execution of the cybersecurity mission, including expediting of information sharing agreements.	
Sec. 6. Cyber Incident Response Plans	
(a) In General	
Amends Sec. 227 of the HSA to change “Plan” to “Plans” in the title, to specify the U/S-CIP as the responsible official, and to add a new subsection:	
‘(b) Updates to the Cyber Incident Annex to the National Response Framework’	
Requires the Secretary, in coordination with other agency heads and in accordance with the National Cybersecurity Incident Response Plan, to update, maintain, and exercise regularly the Cyber Incident Annex to the DHS National Response Framework.	
(b) Clerical Amendment	
Amends the table of contents of the act to reflect the title	
change made by (a).	
Sec. 7. Security and Resiliency of Public Safety Communications; Cybersecurity Awareness Campaign	
(a) In General	
Adds two new sections to the HSA: ‘Sec. 230. Security and Resiliency of Public Safety Communications’ Requires the NCCIC to coordinate with the DHS Office of Emergency Communications to assess information on cybersecurity incidents involving public safety communications to facilitate continuous improvement in those communications.	

NCPAA—H.R. 1731	PCNA—H.R. 1560
'Sec. 231. Cybersecurity Awareness Campaign' '(a) In General' Requires the U/S-CIP to develop and implement an awareness campaign on risks and best practices for mitigation and response, including at a minimum public service announcements and information on best practices that are vendor- and technology-neutral. '(b) Consultation' Requires consultation with a wide range of stakeholders. (b) Clerical Amendment Amends the table of contents of the act to include the new sections. Sec. 8. Critical Infrastructure Protection Research and Development (a) Strategic Plan; Public-Private Consortiums Adds a new section to the HSA: 'Sec. 318. Research and Development Strategy for Critical Infrastructure Protection' '(a) In General' Requires the Secretary to submit to Congress within 180 days of enactment, and biennially thereafter, a strategic plan to guide federal research and development in technology relating to both cyber- and physical security for CI. '(b) Contents of Plan' Requires the plan to include - CI risks and technology gaps identified in consultation with stakeholders and a resulting risk and gap analysis, - prioritized needs based on that analysis, emphasizing technologies to address rapidly evolving threats and technology and including clearly defined roadmaps, - facilities and capabilities required to meet those needs, - current and planned programmatic initiatives to foster technology advancement and deployment, including collaborative opportunities, and - progress on meeting plan requirements. '(c) Coordination' Requires coordination between the DHS Under Secretaries for Science and Technology and for the National Protection and Programs Directorate. [Note: Sec. 5 renames the latter position as the U/S-CIP.]	

Table 1. (Continued)

NCPAA—H.R. 1731	PCNA—H.R. 1560
‘(d) Consultation’ Requires the Under Secretary for Science and Technology to consult with CI Sector Coordinating Councils, heads of other relevant federal agencies, and state, local, and tribal governments as appropriate. (b) Clerical Amendment Amends the table of contents of the act to include the new section. Sec. 9. Report on Reducing Cybersecurity Risks in DHS Data Centers Requires a report to HSC and HSGAC within one year of enactment on the feasibility of creating an environment within DHS for reduction in cybersecurity risks in data centers, including but not limited to increased compartmentalization of systems with a mix of security controls among compartments.	
	Sec. 8. Report on Cybersecurity Threats (a) Report Required Requires the DNI, in consultation with heads of other appropriate elements of the IC, to submit within 180 days of enactment a report to the House and Senate Intelligence Committees on cybersecurity threats, including attacks, theft, and data breaches. (b) Contents Requires that the report include (1) assessments of current U.S. intelligence sharing and cooperation relationships with other countries on such threats directed against the United States and threatening U.S. national security interests, the economy, and intellectual property, identifying the utility of relationships, participation by elements of the IC, and possible improvements, (2) a list and assessment of countries and nonstate actors constituting the primary sources of such threats, (3) description of how much U.S. capabilities to respond to or prevent such

NCPAA—H.R. 1731	PCNA—H.R. 1560
	threats to the U.S. private sector are degraded by delays in notification of the threats, (4) assessment of additional technologies or capabilities that would enhance the U.S. ability to prevent and respond to such threats, and (5) assessment of private-sector technologies or practices that could be rapidly fielded to assist the IC in preventing and responding to such threats. (c) Form of Report Requires that the report be unclassified, but may include a classified annex. (d) Public Availability of Report Requires that the unclassified portion of the report be publicly available. (e) Intelligence Community Defined Defines intelligence community as in 50 USC 3003.
Sec. 10. Assessment	
Requires the Comptroller General, within two years of enactment, to submit a report to HSC and HSGAC assessing implementation of the bill and, as practicable, findings on increased sharing at NCCIC and throughout the United States.	
Sec. 11. Consultation	
Requires a report from the U/S-CIP on "the feasibility of a prioritization plan in the event of simultaneous multi-CI incidents.	
Sec. 12. Technical Assistance	
Requires the DHS IG to review US-CERT and ICS-CERT operations to assess their capacity for responding to current and potentially increasing requests for technical assistance from nonfederal entities.	
Sec. 13. Prohibition on New Regulatory Authority	Sec. 9(l) Regulatory Authority
Stipulates that the bill does not grant DHS new authority to promulgate regulations or set standards relating to cybersecurity for nonfederal, nongovernmental entities.	Stipulates that the bill does not authorize (1) promulgation of regulations or (2) establishment of regulatory authority not specified by the bill, or (3) duplicative or conflicting regulatory actions.

Table 1. (Continued)

NCPAA—H.R. 1731	PCNA—H.R. 1560
Sec. 14 Sunset Ends all requirements for reports in the bill seven years after enactment. Sec. 8. Prohibition on New Funding Stipulates that the bill does not authorize additional funds for implementation and must be carried out using available amounts.	
	Sec. 10. Conforming Amendments Adds information shared under the bill to the kinds of information exempt from disclosure under FOIA.

Source: CRS.
Notes: See "Notes on the Table."

End Notes

[1] The analysis is limited to a textual comparison of the bills and is not intended to reach any legal conclusions regarding them.

[2] The Rules Committee print is available at http://docs.house.gov/billsthisweek/20150420/CPRT-114-HPRT-RU00- HR1731.pdf.

[3] The NCPAA is used as the basis for comparison. This approach was taken for purposes of efficiency and convenience only. CRS does not advocate or take positions on legislation or legislative issues.

[4] The White House, Updated Information Sharing Legislative Proposal, 2015, http://www.whitehouse.gov/sites/default/files/omb/legislative/letters/updated-information-sharing-legislative-proposal.pdf.

[5] Executive Order 13691, "Promoting Private Sector Cybersecurity Information Sharing," Federal Register 80, no. 34 (February 20, 2015): 9349–53, http://www.gpo.gov/fdsys/pkg/FR-2015-02-20/pdf/2015-03714.pdf.

[6] Senate Committee on Homeland Security and Government Affairs, Protecting America from Cyber Attacks: The Importance of Information Sharing, 2015, http://www.hsgac.senate.gov/hearings/protecting-america-from-cyber attacks-the-importance-of-information-sharing. The hearing was not specifically on the White House proposal but it was held after the proposal was submitted and before the introduction of S. 456.

[7] See, for example, CSIS Commission on Cybersecurity for the 44th Presidency, Cybersecurity Two Years Later, January 2011, http://csis.org/files/publication/110128_ Lewis_CybersecurityTwoYearsLater_Web.pdf.

[8] The IC consists of 17 agencies and others as designated under 50 U.S.C. 3003.

[9] The House Committee on Homeland Security held two hearings on the White House proposal before H.R. 1731 was introduced (House Committee on Homeland Security, Examining the President's Cybersecurity Information Sharing Proposal, 2015, http://homeland.house.gov/hearing/hearing-administration-s-cybersecurity-legislative-proposalinformation-sharing; House Committee on Homeland Security, Subcommittee on Cybersecurity, Infrastructure

Protection, and Security Technologies, Industry Perspectives on the President's Cybersecurity Information Sharing Proposal, 2015, http://homeland.house.gov/hearing/ subcommittee-hearing-industry-perspectives-president-scybersecurity-information-sharing).

[10] See, for example, Testimony of Martin C. Libicki before the House Committee on Oversight & Government Reform, Subcommittee on Information Technology, hearing on Industry Perspectives on the President's Cybersecurity Information Sharing Proposal, 2015, http://homeland.house.gov/hearing/subcommittee-hearing-industry-perspectivespresident-s-cybersecurity-information-sharing.

[11] For example, in the Cybersecurity Framework developed by the National Institute of Standards and Technology, target levels of information sharing vary among the four tiers of cybersecurity implementation developed for organizations with different risk profiles (National Institute of Standards and Technology, Framework for Improving Critical Infrastructure Cybersecurity, Version 1.0, February 12, 2014, http://www.nist.gov/ cyberframework/upload/ cybersecurity-framework-021214-final.pdf).

In: Cybersecurity and Cyber-Information Sharing ISBN: 978-1-63483-137-6
Editor: Julia M. Morgan

Chapter 4

EXECUTIVE ORDER 13691: PROMOTING PRIVATE SECTOR CYBERSECURITY INFORMATION SHARING*

Barack Obama

By the authority vested in me as President by the Constitution and the laws of the United States of America, it is hereby ordered as follows:

Section 1. Policy. In order to address cyber threats to public health and safety, national security, and economic security of the United States, private companies, nonprofit organizations, executive departments and agencies (agencies), and other entities must be able to share information related to cybersecurity risks and incidents and collaborate to respond in as close to real time as possible.

Organizations engaged in the sharing of information related to cybersecurity risks and incidents play an invaluable role in the collective cybersecurity of the United States. The purpose of this order is to encourage the voluntary formation of such organizations, to establish mechanisms to continually improve the capabilities and functions of these organizations, and to better allow these organizations to partner with the Federal Government on a voluntary basis.

Such information sharing must be conducted in a manner that protects the privacy and civil liberties of individuals, that preserves business

* This is an edited, reformatted and augmented version of an Executive Order, issued by the White House Office of the Press Secretary, February 13, 2015.

confidentiality, that safeguards the information being shared, and that protects the ability of the Government to detect, investigate, prevent, and respond to cyber threats to the public health and safety, national security, and economic security of the United States.

This order builds upon the foundation established by Executive Order 13636 of February 12, 2013 (Improving Critical Infrastructure Cybersecurity), and Presidential Policy Directive-21 (PPD-21) of February 12, 2013 (Critical Infrastructure Security and Resilience).

Policy coordination, guidance, dispute resolution, and periodic in-progress reviews for the functions and programs described and assigned herein shall be provided through the interagency process established in Presidential Policy Directive-l (PPD-l) of February 13, 2009 (Organization of the National Security Council System), or any successor.

Sec. 2. Information Sharing and Analysis Organizations. (a) The Secretary of Homeland Security (Secretary) shall strongly encourage the development and formation of Information Sharing and Analysis Organizations (ISAOs).

(b) ISAOs may be organized on the basis of sector, sub-sector, region, or any other affinity, including in response to particular emerging threats or vulnerabilities. ISAO membership may be drawn from the public or private sectors, or consist of a combination of public and private sector organizations. ISAOs may be formed as for-profit or nonprofit entities.

(c) The National Cybersecurity and Communications Integration Center (NCCIC), established under section 226(b) of the Homeland Security Act of 2002 (the "Act"), shall engage in continuous, collaborative, and inclusive coordination with ISAOs on the sharing of information related to cybersecurity risks and incidents, addressing such risks and incidents, and strengthening information security systems consistent with sections 212 and 226 of the Act.

(d) In promoting the formation of ISAOs, the Secretary shall consult with other Federal entities responsible for conducting cybersecurity activities, including Sector-Specific Agencies, independent regulatory agencies at their discretion, and national security and law enforcement agencies.

Sec. 3. ISAO Standards Organization. (a) The Secretary, in consultation with other Federal entities responsible for conducting cybersecurity and related activities, shall, through an open and competitive process, enter into an agreement with a nongovernmental organization to serve as the ISAO Standards Organization (SO), which shall identify a common set of voluntary standards or guidelines for the creation and functioning of ISAOs under this order. The standards shall further the goal of creating robust information sharing related to cybersecurity risks and incidents with ISAOs and among

ISAOs to create deeper and broader networks of information sharing nationally, and to foster the development and adoption of automated mechanisms for the sharing of information. The standards will address the baseline capabilities that ISAOs under this order should possess and be able to demonstrate. These standards shall address, but not be limited to, contractual agreements, business processes, operating procedures, technical means, and privacy protections, such as minimization, for ISAO operation and ISAO member participation.

(b) To be selected, the SO must demonstrate the ability to engage and work across the broad community of organizations engaged in sharing information related to cybersecurity risks and incidents, including ISAOs, and associations and private companies engaged in information sharing in support of their customers.

(c) The agreement referenced in section 3(a) shall require that the SO engage in an open public review and comment process for the development of the standards referenced above, soliciting the viewpoints of existing entities engaged in sharing information related to cybersecurity risks and incidents, owners and operators of critical infrastructure, relevant agencies, and other public and private sector stakeholders.

(d) The Secretary shall support the development of these standards and, in carrying out the requirements set forth in this section, shall consult with the Office of Management and Budget, the National Institute of Standards and Technology in the Department of Commerce, Department of Justice, the Information Security Oversight Office in the National Archives and Records Administration, the Office of the Director of National Intelligence, Sector-Specific Agencies, and other interested Federal entities. All standards shall be consistent with voluntary international standards when such international standards will advance the objectives of this order, and shall meet the requirements of the National Technology Transfer and Advancement Act of 1995 (Public Law 104-113), and OMB Circular A-119, as revised.

Sec. 4. Critical Infrastructure Protection Program. (a) Pursuant to sections 213 and 214(h) of the Critical Infrastructure Information Act of 2002, I hereby designate the NCCIC as a critical infrastructure protection program and delegate to it authority to enter into voluntary agreements with ISAOs in order to promote critical infrastructure security with respect to cybersecurity.

(b) Other Federal entities responsible for conducting cybersecurity and related activities to address threats to the public health and safety, national security, and economic security, consistent with the objectives of this order, may participate in activities under these agreements.

(c) The Secretary will determine the eligibility of ISAOs and their members for any necessary facility or personnel security clearances associated with voluntary agreements in accordance with Executive Order 13549 of August 18, 2010 (Classified National Security Information Programs for State, Local, Tribal, and Private Sector Entities), and Executive Order 12829 of January 6, 1993 (National Industrial Security Program), as amended, including as amended by this order.

Sec. 5. Privacy and Civil Liberties Protections. (a) Agencies shall coordinate their activities under this order with their senior agency officials for privacy and civil liberties and ensure that appropriate protections for privacy and civil liberties are incorporated into such activities. Such protections shall be based upon the Fair Information Practice Principles and other privacy and civil liberties policies, principles, and frameworks as they apply to each agency's activities.

(b) Senior privacy and civil liberties officials for agencies engaged in activities under this order shall conduct assessments of their agency's activities and provide those assessments to the Department of Homeland Security (DHS) Chief Privacy Officer and the DHS Office for Civil Rights and Civil Liberties for consideration and inclusion in the Privacy and Civil Liberties Assessment report required under Executive Order 13636.

Sec. 6. National Industrial Security Program. Executive Order 12829, as amended, is hereby further amended as follows:

(a) the second paragraph is amended by inserting "the Intelligence Reform and Terrorism Prevention Act of 2004," after "the National Security Act of 1947, as amended,";

(b) Sec. 101(b) is amended to read as follows: "The National Industrial Security Program shall provide for the protection of information classified pursuant to Executive Order 13526 of December 29, 2009, or any predecessor or successor order, and the Atomic Energy Act of 1954, as amended (42 U.S.C. 2011 *et seq.*).";

(c) Sec. 102(b) is amended by replacing the first paragraph with: "In consultation with the National Security Advisor, the Director of the Information Security Oversight Office, in accordance with Executive Order 13526 of December 29, 2009, shall be responsible for implementing and monitoring the National Industrial Security Program and shall:";

(d) Sec. 102(c) is amended to read as follows: "Nothing in this order shall be construed to supersede the authority of the Secretary of Energy or the Nuclear Regulatory Commission under the Atomic Energy Act of 1954, as amended (42 U.S.C. 2011 *et seq.*), or the authority of the Director of National

Intelligence (or any Intelligence Community element) under the Intelligence Reform and Terrorism Prevention Act of 2004, the National Security Act of 1947, as amended, or Executive Order 12333 of December 8, 1981, as amended, or the authority of the Secretary of Homeland Security, as the Executive Agent for the Classified National Security Information Program established under Executive Order 13549 of August 18, 2010 (Classified National Security Information Program for State, Local, Tribal, and Private Sector Entities).";

(e) Sec. 201(a) is amended to read as follows: "The Secretary of Defense, in consultation with all affected agencies and with the concurrence of the Secretary of Energy, the Nuclear Regulatory Commission, the Director of National Intelligence, and the Secretary of Homeland Security, shall issue and maintain a National Industrial Security Program Operating Manual (Manual). The Secretary of Energy and the Nuclear Regulatory Commission shall prescribe and issue that portion of the Manual that pertains to information classified under the Atomic Energy Act of 1954, as amended (42 U.S.C. 2011 *et seq*.). The Director of National Intelligence shall prescribe and issue that portion of the Manual that pertains to intelligence sources and methods, including Sensitive Compartmented Information. The Secretary of Homeland Security shall prescribe and issue that portion of the Manual that pertains to classified information shared under a designated critical infrastructure protection program.";

(f) Sec. 201(f) is deleted in its entirety;

(g) Sec. 201(e) is redesignated Sec. 201(f) and revised by substituting "Executive Order 13526 of December 29, 2009, or any successor order," for "Executive Order No. 12356 of April 2, 1982.";

(h) Sec. 201(d) is redesignated Sec. 201(e) and revised by substituting "the Director of National Intelligence, and the Secretary of Homeland Security" for "and the Director of Central Intelligence.";

(i) a new Sec. 201(d) is inserted after Sec. 201(c) to read as follows: "The Manual shall also prescribe arrangements necessary to permit and enable secure sharing of classified information under a designated critical infrastructure protection program to such authorized individuals and organizations as determined by the Secretary of Homeland Security.";

(j) Sec. 202(b) is amended to read as follows: "The Director of National Intelligence retains authority over access to intelligence sources and methods, including Sensitive Compartmented Information. The Director of National Intelligence may inspect and monitor contractor, licensee, and grantee programs and facilities that involve access to such information or may enter into written agreements with the Secretary of Defense, as Executive Agent, or with the Director of the Central Intelligence Agency to inspect and monitor these programs or facilities, in whole or in part, on the Director's behalf.";

(k) Sec. 202(d) is redesignated as Sec. 202(e); and

(l) in Sec. 202 a new subsection (d) is inserted after subsection (c) to read as follows: "The Secretary of Homeland Security may determine the eligibility for access to Classified National Security Information of contractors, licensees, and grantees and their respective employees under a designated critical infrastructure protection program, including parties to agreements with such program; the Secretary of Homeland Security may inspect and monitor contractor, licensee, and grantee programs and facilities or may enter into written agreements with the Secretary of Defense, as Executive Agent, or with the Director of the Central Intelligence Agency, to inspect and monitor these programs or facilities in whole or in part, on behalf of the Secretary of Homeland Security."

Sec. 7. Definitions. (a) "Critical infrastructure information" has the meaning given the term in section 212(3) of the Critical Infrastructure Information Act of 2002.

(b) "Critical infrastructure protection program" has the meaning given the term in section 212(4) of the Critical Infrastructure Information Act of 2002.

(c) "Cybersecurity risk" has the meaning given the term in section 226(a)(1) of the Homeland Security Act of 2002 (as amended by the National Cybersecurity Protection Act of 2014).

(d) "Fair Information Practice Principles" means the eight principles set forth in Appendix A of the National Strategy for Trusted Identities in Cyberspace.

(e) "Incident" has the meaning given the term in section 226(a)(2) of the Homeland Security Act of 2002 (as amended by the National Cybersecurity Protection Act of 2014).

(f) "Information Sharing and Analysis Organization" has the meaning given the term in section 212(5) of the Critical Infrastrucure Information Act of 2002.

(g) "Sector-Specific Agency" has the meaning given the term in PPD-21, or any successor.

Sec. 8. General Provisions. (a) Nothing in this order shall be construed to impair or otherwise affect:

(i) the authority granted by law or Executive Order to an agency, or the head thereof; or

(ii) the functions of the Director of the Office of Management and Budget relating to budgetary, administrative, or legislative proposals.

(b) This order shall be implemented consistent with applicable law and subject to the availability of appropriations. Nothing in this order shall be construed to alter or limit any authority or responsibility of an agency under existing law including those activities conducted with the private sector relating to criminal and national security threats. Nothing in this order shall be construed to provide an agency with authority for regulating the security of critical infrastructure in addition to or to a greater extent than the authority the agency has under existing law.

(c) All actions taken pursuant to this order shall be consistent with requirements and authorities to protect intelligence and law enforcement sources and methods.

(d) This order is not intended to, and does not, create any right or benefit, substantive or procedural, enforceable at law or in equity by any party against the United States, its departments, agencies, or entities, its officers, employees, or agents, or any other person.

BARACK OBAMA

THE WHITE HOUSE,
February 13, 2015.

INDEX

C

D

E

F

G

L

M

N

O

P

Q

R

S

T